Hemkunt

Hemkunt

A Journey
From the Past to the Present

Col. Avtar Singh Berar

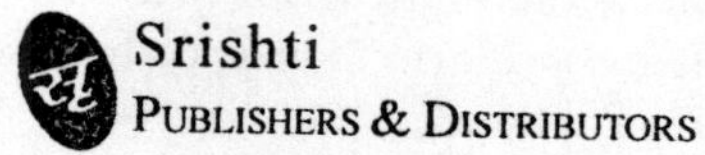
Srishti
PUBLISHERS & DISTRIBUTORS

SRISHTI PUBLISHERS & DISTRIBUTORS
64-A, Adhchini
Sri Aurobindo Marg
New Delhi 110 017
srishtipublishers@yahoo.com

First published by SRISHTI PUBLISHERS & DISTRIBUTORS in 2003

Rs. 195.00
ISBN 81-88575-15-1

Cover design by
Creative Concept
40/223, C R Park
New Delhi 110 019

Typeset in AGaramond 11pt. by Skumar at Srishti

Dedicated to

Pandit Tara Har Narottam

Who discovered Hemkunt in 1884

and

To all the dedicated yatris

Who undertake this difficult journey

To pay homage to Dusht Daman

Contents

Preface

One morning, early in the year 1990, as I stepped out of the local gurudwara of Hargobind Enclave, the melodious tunes and the profound words of the shabad kirtan still resounding in my mind I chanced upon this poster announcing the pilgrimage to Hemkunt Sahib. It read that Bhai Dharti Dhakel Singh was leading a jatha on foot to Hemkunt Sahib, at a height of 15,200 feet! I was 60 years old. But at that moment of time, the poster seemed to be there just for me. I could not resist the call in spite of all the odds and decided to take up the challenge and join the jatha.

There were about a hundred men, women and children in all. We assembled in gurudwara Damdama Sahib, New Delhi on 25 May 1990. We covered the distance of about five hundred kilometres and reached Hemkunt Sahib on June the fourteenth, which happened to be the day of Sangrand. The journey was a treat in itself, but while walking lots of questions surfaced in my mind. Questions regarding the authenticity of the place and the writings that proclaim it; questions about reincarnation and memory of previous births; questions concerned with the tenth master with whom the place is associated. Why, for instance, did he not visit the place? Why did he not include his own writings in the *Guru Granth Sahib*? Why did he choose to put them down in a separate book, the *Dasam Granth*, and why has the common man lost sight of this granth? The questions were many and there were no answers. I asked everyone to throw some light on the issues in my mind and satisfy my curiosity. But no one seemed to know more than me. At Gobind Ghat, I searched the library for books on the subject of Hemkunt Sahib. A few pamphlets, more like travel guides, were available but none answered my questions. That is when I decided to go deep into the subject, do some research and put it down in a book for those who, like me, would be interested in knowing more about the place, its history and its background. I was advised against it because it is a controversial subject, I was told.

In 1997, I went to Kailash Mansarovar, in Tibet. It was a thirty-day trip arranged by the Ministry of External Affairs. On my return I wrote a book titled *Kailash Mansarovar - Thirty Days of Adventure and Ecstasy* in English and *Kailash Mansarovar di Param Yatra* in Punjabi. Both the books were well-received. I decided to write a book on Hemkunt Sahib. I started collecting information from wherever I could get it. In every book that I read one name came up again and again. The name of Pandit Tara Har Narotam, and his book *Guru Tirath Sangrah*. I looked for this book in all the bookshops as well as in all the important libraries in Delhi. But it was not to be found anywhere. I asked people and went wherever they sent me, but always returned disappointed. Finally after about three years of going round in circles, I managed to lay my hands on an old copy. I photocopied the entire book and took it home to study it in detail. I was deeply impressed by the tremendous effort made by Pandit Tara Har Narottam to search for the place, and equally surprised that no one deemed it fit to follow it up.

Slowly and gradually the material on Hemkunt began to increase and the book in my mind started to take shape. I went to Kanpur and Rishikesh and met lots of people from Hemkunt Trust but no information was forthcoming. It seems the

Hemkunt Trust have not kept any records. This book is thus incomplete; it is only the beginning of writing on the subject. If there is anyone who has more information please pass it on to me or to the Hemkunt Trust so that it is available for further research.

I have tried to trace the background of Hemkunt Sahib, its significance to the Sikhs, and the long story of the search for this place, and subsequently the construction of the gurudwara. I have tried to depict the correct story after consulting books available on the subject and interviewing lots of persons concerned with it. If due to some reason it is not acceptable to someone, I apologize in advance, and would welcome constructive suggestions and more information.

My thanks to Sardar Devinder Singh Toki who was my guide-philosopher in writing this book. He helped me at every stage to make this project feasable. I am grateful to my wife Manjit, who went through the first draft and gave valuable suggestions, and Satjit Wadva who edited and reorganised it. I am most grateful to Sardar M. S. Siali who allowed me to use material and photographs from his book *Gurudwara in the Himalayas*.

Col A. S. Berar (Retd.)

hemkunt

Beauty Beyond Compare

Talk to any Sikh returning from Hemkunt Sahib and he may well relate a few unbelievably strange stories. They may be pure imagination but are understandable after an experience of the place, which is very much a part of this world but has the power to transport you into another world. Myth, mystery, miracles make this place a unique phenomenon. Beauty unimaginable and unheard of hits you in the eye. Snow-covered peaks ablaze with clear bright sunshine sweep you off your feet. Crystal clear water of the icy cold pond, Hemkunt, reflecting the blue sky with white clouds floating in it, brings you so close to the heavens that you feel you could touch them if you stretched your arms. And in the midst of sheer nature stands the gurudwara, a tribute to the effort of mortal man, a salutation to the indomitable will that knows no barriers in the face of conviction.

At a height of 4320 m above sea level lies this lake surrounded by mountains on three sides. It takes five to seven days journey through the Himalayas to get there. The entire route, Gobind Marg is strewn with gurudwaras where the devotees rest overnight to continue their pilgrimmage to Hemkunt. All their needs are catered to with infinite dedication and spirit of service. No small wonder then to see stars in daylight when you reach the highest peak and the shrine. A dip in the icy cold water makes you warm, the clouds above seem to float beneath you in the water, the air lifts you up to a different level of consciousness, and when someone, tall and imposing, attired in a navy blue robe and turban, shows you the way, you wonder why your companion walking beside you did not see a thing.

Ancient scriptures have mentioned this place as a holy place because of the holy men who prayed and worshipped at this scenic spot. Lord Krishna and Arjun are said to have been there. Researchers have also found that Guru Nanak visited the place in one of his odysseys. But the place is closely related to the tenth and last guru, Guru Gobind Singh.

And that is the most mysterious connection, for it connects his previous birth to the present one. He claims to have meditated on this spot for a very long time, long before he was born in the house of Guru Tegh Bahadur. His tapasya bore fruit and he became one with the Almighty. He had no need to come again to this world but the Lord instructed him to take another birth and he was born as the tenth and last guru to bear the torch of Guru Nanak.

That this place was the favorite haunt of many holy men is evident in every inch of the place. The whole valley is charged with their vibes. The moment you land there you seem to be taken to another world. The experience has to be felt. It defies description. The fatigue, the exhaustion after an arduous steep climb just evaporates. You feel a new strength in your limbs and a new energy pulsates in your veins. There is lightness in your step that you have never felt before. You could sing and dance. You could fly. And the vastness of the Himalayas fills your heart and expands you so much that you could embrace the whole universe.

If there is a place on earth that can give you an experience of the other world, it is Hemkunt. It is a miracle in itself. Everyone returning from the pilgrimage to Hemkunt feels he has touched that space within him which is of the beyond. The body transcends its boundaries to meet the soul as the earth raises itself to touch the stars through these lofty peaks.

To the scientific mind, it is easy to explain. The high altitude, the lack of oxygen in the desired measure, the long and arduous journey, all put together can change the chemistry of the body and one can go into a trance. And it is easy to see things not really there. To the poetic mind it is the beauty of the place that holds the power to work on the imagination of man. But to the devotee, it is divine. There is God in every stone and pebble, in the very freshness of the air and in the whiteness of the snow. God is everywhere no doubt, but here is a place that makes His presence palpable. You could touch it and be blessed.

Hemkunt is not just a place. It is a dream come true. A quest fulfilled. A goal achieved. Every Sikh hopes to have this experience at least once in his lifetime. Strangely his appetite for more and more visits increases after he has been there once.

The mountains beckon and the guru seems to walk a hundred miles to meet you half way.

Charan sharan gur ek painda jaye chal
Satgur kot painda aagey hoi let hai

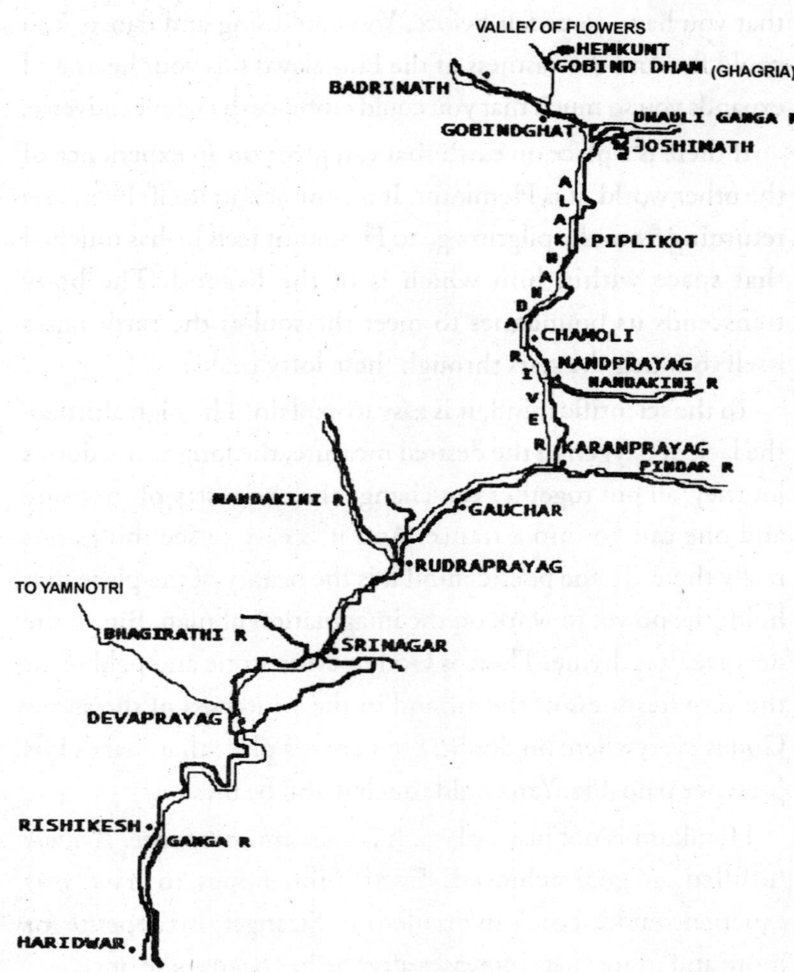

The route from Haridwar to Hemkunt and Badrinath. Not to scale.

the pilgrimage

Charan Chalo Marg Gobind
Sukhmani Sahib

Devotees may come from any part of the world, but they all start their journey from Hardwar. Shubh-arambh. An auspicious beginning. Haridwar means the door to meet Hari, God. It is an ancient town, washed by the water of the holiest of rivers in India, the Ganges. Ganga. It falls in Garhwal region, now in the new state of Uttaranchal. This province has many ancient holy places of the Hindus. Badrinath, Kedarnath, Gangotri, Yamnotri all fall in Garhwal. Pilgrims have been going to these places from times immemorial, when there were just paths, and no roads and no transport. The Sikhs are the latest entrants who generally go to Hemkunt specifically, but many of them visit all the other shrines also. Most of them start their journey from Hardwar, after taking a dip in the Ganges.

First Halt
HARDWAR

Hardwar is located on the branch line of Laksar-Dehradun. It is connected to not only the metropolitan cities, but to various towns in Uttar Pradesh, Punjab, Haryana and Himachal Pradesh. The city is overcrowded, and overflowing with tourists and visitors. Foreigners in various shades of saffron, with foreheads smeared with sandalwood paste are a common sight. One can get a bus for any town in the neighbouring states at any time. So there is no difficulty in reaching this place to begin a journey to the valley of gods.

Hardwar is situated on the banks of the Ganges. After roaring down from the mountains, the river, better known as the Ganga, becomes calm and placid when it enters the plains at Rishikesh. Starting from Gaumukh, Gangotri, the Ganga cuts across the breadth of India and finally merges in the Bay of Bengal at Ganga Sagar, near Calcutta. All along the Gangetic plain the soil is rich and fertile, and many important towns of northern India are

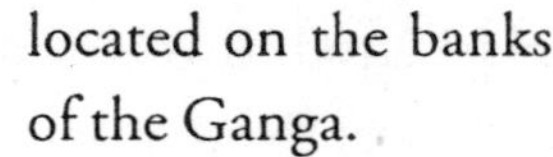

located on the banks of the Ganga.

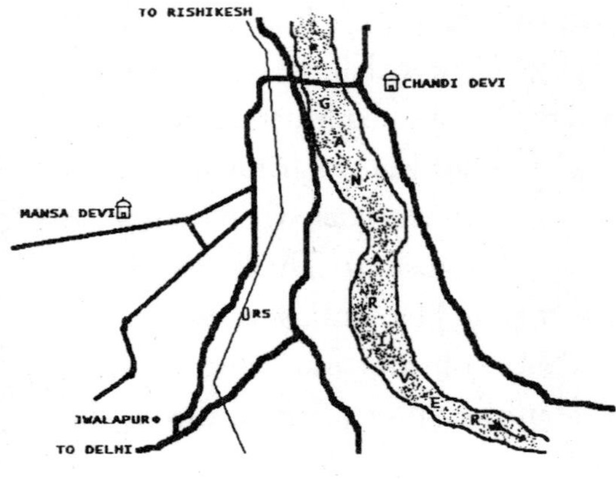

Hardwar is full of spacious dharamshalas and ashrams. They are the main source of income of the local people, as all tourists and pilgrims need to stay overnight in Hardwar to proceed on their journey to the various holy places, and other tourist spots. It is easy to get accommodation in any one of them. Some sadhus offer accommodation in their 'akharas' and tell the pilgrims of the glory of their sect.

Guru Nanak visited Hardwar on his first 'udasi', journey. The incident that happened there was an eye-opener for all present, and a lesson for posterity. A large crowd of people were standing in the Ganga and were offering water to the sun. He also went there and started doing the same, but in the opposite direction. They were surprised and asked him the reason for his act. In reply he asked to be told why they were offering water to the sun. They said that they were offering water to their ancestors who had died long ago. The Guru said that he was sending water to his fields in Kartarpur in Punjab. They laughed at him and asked how he hoped to reach the water to his land so far away. He said that if water could reach their ancestors in another world, then why not his fields which were only a few hundred miles away. The lesson was brought home to them in his quiet manner. Rituals and meaningless traditions find no place in the Sikh way of life. A small gurudwara was built at Har Ki Pauri to commemorate his visit and the incident. It is managed by the pandas, the brahmin priests, but hardly anyone visits it.

Pilgrims come enroute to the holy places throughout the year but Hardwar is famous for the Kumbh Mela – the fair that is held once in twelve years, and Ardh Kumbh Mela, after every six years. People from all over India and abroad throng this place in great numbers. Normally, one of the cabinet ministers or a minister of state is deputed to look after the arrangements. In spite of all the arrangements there are many shortcomings. Many mishaps and accidents take place, because every one wants to take a dip in the holy water at the auspicious time. It is believed that taking a dip in the holy Ganga at an astrologically prescribed time will wash away all one's sins. Hence the race for a bath. It causes stampedes and many accidents occur. In the midst of all the confusion it is often observed that the custodians of law and order are the ones who make the confusion worse because special arrangements have to be made for them.

After taking a dip in the river, pilgrims go sight-seeing and visiting places of religious interest.

But in the evening they all converge at Har Ki Pauri to participate in the Arti, the evening prayer. Thousands of earthen lamps are lighted and gently slipped into the Ganga to float on the dancing waves. The lit lamps and their reflection in the water is a sight worth seeing. It is as if the river of lights is dancing to the tune of the shrill sounds of shankhs, conch shells, and bells. The stars above and lamps below, all seem to join in the arti. And one feels part of the whole, and closer to the deity. The whole scene is breathtaking. Many people visit Hardwar just to participate in the arti.

Har Ki Pauri is next to Brahm Kund, which is believed to be the first step towards God. In the battle of Mahabharat millions of people died and their ashes were immersed in the river at Har Ki Pauri. Since then it has been customary for the Hindus and Sikhs to immerse the mortal remains of their near and dear ones at this spot. Earlier Sikhs used to come here, but after being cheated by the wily pandas, they started to immerse the remains at Sri Kiratpur Sahib, situated on the bank of river Sutlej. Guru Amar Das, when he was not converted to Sikhism, had visited this place twenty-two times for worship. A magnificient gurudwara has been constructed in his memory in the house of a panda where he used to come and stay. This gurudwara is near Kankhal on the bank of the river, and the remains of the dead can be immersed here.

There are many religious and industrial places situated in and around Hardwar.

Mata Mansa Devi Temple is on top of a hill. Earlier people used to scale the steep climb to seek the blessings of Mata Mansa Devi. But now it is connected with a ropeway, which is 546 metres in length. One gets there in a very short time. A panoramic view of the city with the Ganga flowing in the middle is a treat for the eyes.

Gurukul Kangri University is situated on the Hardwar Jawalpur Road and is about four kilometres from Hardwar. Ayurvedic medicines are prepared here and supplied all over India. Hundreds of students study this ancient stream of medicine and are awarded degrees.

Bharat Heavy Electricals is a public sector undertaking situated near Jawalpur town. Heavy electrical motors (generators) are manufactured for home consumption as well as made to order and exported to various countries.

Earlier the devotees on their way to Hemkunt used to stay in various dharamshalas as there were no gurudwaras. Bhai Ram Singh Jharuwale who belonged to Garhwal used to bring large groups of pilgrim jathas, for Hemkunt darshan. Once when he brought a very big group, he did not find any place for them to stay the night in any dharamshala. He decided to build a dharamshala. He purchased a piece of land in Nirmala Chauny

(Cantonment) near Hardwar Railway Station, and constructed a dharamshala there. In 1984, he donated the land and building to Hemkunt Trust. The Trust purchased adjoining land and constructed a big gurudwara and named it Gurudwara Hemkunt Sahib Trust. Very few people are aware of the existence of this gurudwara or what is considered to be the starting point of the pilgrimage to Hemkunt. It is not very well connected by road and the buses have to take a circuitous route to reach this place. So they avoid it and head directly for the Rishikesh Gurudwara which is located at a very convenient place. Sikhs who are not desirous of taking a dip in the Ganges normally skip Hardwar. Since very few Sikh yatris come here, there is no great rush and people can stay here in comfort. The management of the gurudwara is very good.

Second Halt
RISHIKESH

Rishikesh is situated on the bank of river Ganges at a height of 1300 ft above sea level and is at a distance of 25 km from Hardwar. It is considered to be a holy town because of its vicinity to the Ganges, the holiest river in India. As it enters this place the Ganges gives up its tumultuous fury and becomes a very gentle, quiet and peaceful river spreading its banks wide to allow the devotees to pay their homage at various spots. The city is the abode of ancient sages, the rishis and munis. That is where it gets its name. There are many ashrams and yoga centres in the city. It has become a centre of yoga, known all over the world.

It is a fairly large town and is always buzzing with activity, mainly related to tourists and tourism. It is the last railway station on the Hardwar Rishikesh branch line.

There are many places worth visiting here, but the most famous is Lakshman Jhula, a suspension bridge on the river Ganges, suspended by thick steel ropes tied to underground fittings. It was built for the use of pedestrians and mules only, but nowadays even two wheeler scooters can be seen on it. It is said that Lakshman, the younger brother of Sri Ram Chandra performed tapasya here and the bridge was named after him. Originally a wooden bridge, it was converted to a suspension bridge in 1929. Another way of crossing the river is by motor boat, which is an experience in itself. On this side of the river one can visit Lakshman Mandir, Gita Bhawan and Swarg Ashram. Bharat Temple is also very famous.

Rishikesh is at a distance of 230 km from Delhi, and one can easily cover this distance in six to seven hours by bus or car. Those who come from Punjab take the Paonta Sahib and Dehradun route. It is basically from Rishikesh that the journey to Badrinath, Kedarnath, Gangotri and Yamnotri and Hemkunt begins, because many people prefer to start from here.

Prior to 1968, yatris for Hemkunt used to stay at the premises of the Punjab Sindh Kshetra since there was no gurudwara. Here they would change buses. The bigger buses had to be changed for smaller buses which plied in the hilly terrain. In those days pilgrims had to be inoculated against cholera to get permission to proceed further. Those were also the days for one-way traffic because the roads were very narrow. They followed a gate system whereby traffic from one way had to wait till traffic from the other direction had passed. In a convoy the first vehicle, generally a truck would carry a red flag and the last vehicle a green flag. Only when the bus bearing the green flag reached the post was the convoy allowed to move. It took many days extra to complete the journey in those days.

Since then the government has widened the roads and traffic moves comfortably in both directions. Incidentally, the gate system is still followed between Joshimath and Badrinath.

In 1964, almost 50 acres of land was purchased from one Shri Ram Murthy by the Hemkunt Trust. Locals wondered what they would do with such a big plot. Soon they saw the construction of a huge gurudwara start. This gurudwara was built with the intention of accommodating the growing numbers of pilgrims to Hemkunt sahib. The construction of the gurudwara started under the supervision of Sardar Gurbax Singh Bindra, who is currently the President of the Hemkunt Trust.

Born in 1912, he migrated to Rishikesh after the partition of India. He was enthusiastic about advocating the need for a gurudwara and forming the Hemkunt Trust and is one of the founder members.

Gurudwara Rishikesh under construction

The gurudwara is located on the main road to Lakshman Jhula. The complex is not just the gurudwara but has a fairly large sarai, an inn which provides lodging to the pilgrims.

Besides all the essential infrastructure of a gurudwara there is also a missionary school. It was originally intended to construct a double-storeyed gurudwara but now it is multi-storeyed and not just one building but many in the huge complex. There is a big darbar hall on the first floor which has an impressive decor and a fine wooden ceiling. The darbar hall reverbrates with the voice of the granthi and the raagis. The pilgrims join in the recitation of prayers and singing of gurbani. An equally big langar hall and an administrative block is on the ground floor.

Over the years many other buildings have come up to accommodate the yatris. Approximately 4000 yatris can be accommodated at a time. There is plenty of space for parking cars and buses, which is a boon in the congested town. A 101 feet high Nishan Sahib is installed which was donated by Sardar Mohan Singh, one of the trustees, as an offering. On 16 September 1964, the foundation stone was laid for the sarovar and it was completed in record time. It is named Guru Nanak sarovar.

Records show that Bhai Gyan Singh devoted himself to the construction of the gurudwara with his heart and soul. When the accommodation fell short he undertook to build a five-storeyed modern building on the banks of the sarovar. A true karamyogi, a Kar Sewak, he bore all the expenses himself. In 1984, during the Sikh carnage, attempts were made to destroy the gurudwara. But a handful of Sikhs resisted the onslaughts of the mob. The gurudwara suffered minor damage which was repaired at once.

In 1975, the Trust opened a school to teach gurbani. Gurmat Sangeet Bal Vidyalya. It was meant for children from the nearby hills. Children in the age group of 12 to 15 who had basic education upto junior school, were admitted. Baba Gurmukh Singh of Ludhiana provided all the musical instruments and books, and continues to do so even now.

In 1992, a new building was constructed to serve as a hostel for the children. Almost a hundred children are admitted every year. They have to go through a five-year course. Basic education is in Punjabi. The emphasis is on Sikh history and gurmat music. Education is completely free and all the expenses are borne by the Trust. Children who have passed from this school have become famous raagis and are in great demand in foreign countries. Some have even become millionaires now. Students impress the pilgrims with their capacity to recite gurbani and sing mellifluously.

The main aim of this school is to educate the poor locals and make them financially independent. From what they gain in this school it is often noticed that they imbibe the Sikh way of life readily and willingly.

The Sikh pilgrims to Hemkunt Sahib generally travel in chartered buses or their own vehicles, but those who do not come in groups take the local buses to reach Gobind Ghat. The local buses carrying the Hemkunt bound passengers start at 4 o'clock in the morning so that they can reach Badrinath by evening. Gobind Ghat is just a few kilometres short of Badrinath. All the buses stop at the main gate of the gurudwara to pick up passengers.

Third Halt
SRINAGAR

At the Rishikesh Gurudwara activity begins at 2 in the early morning. At amrit vela. All the yatris who are heading for Hemkunt have to be seated in the buses by 4 a.m. There is much hustle and bustle everywhere, especially in the toilets and in the langar hall. They have to leave as early as possible because the journey ahead is long and arduous. They must allow for roadblocks caused by landslides during the rainy season which is actually the only time permitted for the pilgrimage. The season is between June and October for making this pilgrimage and these are the months when it rains most of the time in the hills. Those people who cannot start early have to halt at Srinagar for the night, before proceeding to Joshimath.

After getting ready for the journey the pilgrims arrange their bags in the buses and go to the langar hall for a hot cup of tea and light breakfast. All the gurudwaras on this route have tea served round the clock. Self service is the rule. They pick up their glasses and thalis, eat and drink as much as they want, then clean their utensils so they are ready for the others. After a brief ardas, prayer for a safe journey, they occupy their seats in the bus. Loud jaikaras of 'Bole so nihal – Sat Sri Akal' resound in the gurudwara complex. In the buses they start recting the prayers and singing shabad kirtan.

At a distance of 30 km from Rishikesh there is a town called Biasi, or Viasi, on the banks of the Ganges. When there was the gate system, this used to be the first halt. It is a beautiful and quiet place surrounded by a thick jungle. It is known for its dhabas, the roadside food stalls, which serve hot stuffed parathas for breakfast. Most yatris have breakfast here. The devout pilgrims who undertake this journey on foot, usually stop here for the night. There is no dharamshala or resting place. One has to sleep in the shops, if permitted, or else in the open. They must also carry water with them, because about four kilometres from Biasi begins a very dry mountain terrain, which is the most difficult part of the journey.

From here the hazardous hill journey starts. The road and river criss-cross many times. Sometimes the road rises to the top of the hill leaving the river down below. At other places they run parallel. One gets engrossed in the games they seem to be playing with each other. Teasing and challenging each other. The road runs precariously balanced between the deep gorge on one side and the tall and mighty mountains on the other. At such times one bows his head in reverence and gratitude to those who were instrumental in building these roads. What hardships they must have borne to make the journey easier and more comfortable.

One sees the river in its various moods. If it is a narrow gorge the water comes roaring and rushing furiously. And when it is rocky the water strikes against the rocks sending foam up like a cloud. Whatever the mood it is enchanting to watch the view. When the buses pass over the bridge the river seems to be timid, but the next moment may make one think otherwise. The Ganges in the rainy season is a power to reckon with.

Driving on hill roads is not easy and the maximum speed is about 30 kmph. Even expert drivers have to be very very alert. Though there are enough signboards and signals to warn you of the impending 'U' turns and blind bends, there is no one who can predict the sudden landslides or falling of huge stones on the road.

It takes about three hours for the bus to cover a distance of 71 km, to reach Dev Prayag. Prayag means confluence of two holy rivers. This is a very important meeting point of two rivers – Bhagirathi and Alakhnanda. It is after the union of these two rivers that the river gets the name Ganga.

With the meeting of Bhagirathi and Alakhnanda, Dev Prayag looks like a triangle. Since the sangam is far below the road level, the passengers get a bird's eye view of the confluence. Hundreds of Hindu yatris stop at Dev Prayag to take a dip at the sangam but the Sikhs usually enjoy the scene and proceed on their journey. There are bridges on each river.

Dev Prayag is at a height of 618 m (2000 ft) above sea level. There are two famous temples, one of Raghunath, in memory of Sri Ram Chandra, and the second of Shiv. About the Raghunath temple, it is said, that after conquering Ravana, Rama stopped here to pray for forgiveness for killing a brahmin, and for the atonement of his soul and those of all the brave warriors who laid down their lives in the battlefield. There are two black deities in the temple. Shankaracharya's cave is located near the temple. Raghunath Kirti Mahavidyalya is also located here which is the headquarters of Badrinath Rawal (priests). They are trained in this institute.

From Dev Prayag the road bifurcates. One goes to Yamnotri along the river Bhagirathi, and the other goes to Srinagar along the river Alakhnanda. There is a PWD rest house, many travellers' homes and dharamshalas on this route. Yatris on foot can rest in any one of them and stay overnight.

After about four hours of a non-stop journey, the bus crosses the Alakhnanda at Kirtinagar and reaches Srinagar (Garhwal). Since another very famous city called Srinagar is in Kashmir, this place is called Srinagar Garhwal. Hemkunt Management Trust Gurudwara is located in this town. There are proper arrangements for accommodation for about 600 yatris at a time. Langar is served round the clock. It is a relatively small gurudwara, built in a narrow lane in linear form. The living quarters of the caretakers and granthis are built all around the main building of the gurudwara. Very often the yatris have to spend the night here when they get stranded because of landslides or roadblocks.

Srinagar is a very old city, built by Raja Kanakpal in the fourteenth century. Thereafter Raja Ajaypal made it the capital of Tehri state. It remained the capital till 1803. In 1804, Gorkhas from Nepal invaded the capital. Maharani Salana, the ruling queen, sought the help of the British to drive the invaders out. Tehri Garhwal remained an independent state unlike other parts of Garhwal and Kumaon.

At a height of 579 m (1900 ft) above sea level, this old city is closely connected to Sikh history. In 1517, Guru Nanak visited this city during one of his journeys. A gurudwara named Charan Padhak was constructed in this old town where the Guru stayed. In 1893, the dam on Mahana Lake burst and the whole town was washed away alongwith the gurudwara. There was a great loss of life and property. The new town was then built at a higher altitude.

In the olden days Udasi Sadhus used to stay in this town. They had two hand-written Dasam Granths, with 1540 and 1312 pages respectively. An old woman used to read them once in a while. Most of the time they remained stored in boxes. Then a Sindhi family took these granths home and paid proper respect to them. In 1966, when Hemkunt Trust purchased the land and constructed the gurudwara, these granths were presented to the gurudwara, and one can have darshan of these granths.

In 1970, this place was flooded again, but there was no loss to the new city which is located at a greater height. Srinagar is famous for the Garhwal School of Painting. On 1 December, 1973, the foundation stone of Garhwal University was laid. Many colleges are affiliated to this university. From here one road leads to Pauri and then to Kotdwar, a rail head.

Fourth Halt
JOSHIMATH

Joshimath is 150 km from Srinagar (Garhwal). In normal weather the bus takes about five hours to cover this distance. But this road has to face the vagaries of the weather and the buses have to often encounter landslides and roadblocks. The continuous drizzle which makes the mountains look more enigmatic and enchanting, is actually the most dangerous phenomenon. It loosens the soil and washes it on to the roads, creating a slush on the road. Motor vehicles find it extremely difficult to manoeuvre as there is the risk of skidding. Moreover the road also gives way at many places due to the continuous drizzle.

Sometimes it takes more than two hours to clear a roadblock, and there can be many such blocks on the way. Small vehicles do manage to pass or take a detour, but the bigger vehicles get stuck for long hours. Sometimes, people have to spend the night midway in the chill of the mountain air. And it is usually raining. If one can rise above the physical discomforts, one gets to see the beauty of nature in abundance. At the end of it one is grateful to nature to get an opportunity to see the beauty in detail, which would have been missed in the moving bus.

It is a common sight to see the yatris cooking food on the roadside while chanting Gurbani kirtan.

Rudra Paryag is 34 km from Srinagar and this distance is covered in one hour. It is situated at a height of 610 m (2000 ft) above sea level. Two rivers Alaknanda and Mandakini meet here. Alakhnanda, comes from Badrinath side and the second one, Mandakini originates from Kedar Nath. From here one road branches off to Kedar Nath. There is an ancient temple in this city where the deity is Jagdamba Devi, which is one of the other names of Durga. Even Naradmuni is said to have worshipped in this temple and learnt classical music with the grace of Shivji.

Here Shivji is also worshipped in the name of Rudra Nath. Three mountain districts of Pauri, Tehri and Chamoli meet here. There are a lot of dharamshalas in this town. This is the fourth halt for the yatris who undertake the yatra on foot from Rishikesh.

Gochar, a small town, is next to Rudra Prayag and is situated on a meadow. Gochar, in fact, means pasture. There is an Air Force helipad here and a government hospital.

Karan Prayag is the next town on this road, 32 km from Rudra Prayag, at a height of 788 m above sea level. This town is named after Karan, the worshipper of the Sun God, who played an important role in *Mahabharat.* Two rivers, Pindar Ganga which originates from Pindar glacier and Alakhnanda meet here. If the sky is clear and visibility normal, one can have a view of mountain peaks named Trimul, Donagiri, and Naradbunti. From here one road bifurcates for Ranikhet 135 km away. A Khalsa hotel is located on the main road which is a very old and reputed one. A P.W.D. rest house is located on the bank of river Pindar. One mule track leads to Baij Nath. This is the fifth stop for yatris who are on foot.

After traveling another 21 km, one reaches Nand Prayag where the Nandkini river meets Alakhnanda. Nandkini originates from a glacier near Nanda Devi. At a distance of 10 km, one reaches Chamoli which is situated at a height of 960 m above sea level and is the District Headquarters. This district was carved out from Pauri District after the Indo-China war in 1962. Earlier the metaled road used to end here and one was supposed to undertake the further journey on foot. As usual, there are many dharamshalas located here, and the Gopinath temple is very famous.

From here one road goes to Kedarnath via Tungnath, a very ancient city. The Katori dynasty ruled in this area from the 3rd century to the 14th century. A town called Gopeshwar is just above Chamoli on the hillock and one can have a good view of it from the bus.

In the olden days, when the pilgrims used to undertake the journey to four holy places, there were small huts along the road, called Chattis, where the pilgrims used to stay for a night and could buy rations and cook meals. With the construction of the road, these Chattis have now been converted into hotels and one can find them throughout on this route.

Pipalkoti is located at a distance of 18 km from Chamoli and is at a height of 1219 m above sea level. By hill standards, this is a fairly big town and there are dharamshalas for the pilgrims. Kali Kamliwale's dharamshalas are very famous. A P.W.D. rest house is also located here. Though at a distance of 48 km from Karan Prayag, it is a good halt for yatris on foot. This place is famous for bamboo baskets in different shapes and sizes which are very handy to carry, and tourists love to buy them. If the sky is very clear at night, one is reminded of Guru Nanak Dev's famous shabad "*Gagan mein thal rav chand Deepak bane tarika mandal janak moti.*" There are millions of glittering stars and it seems that if one raises one's hand a bit higher one could catch a star.

From here Joshimath is just 16 km but this is a very tricky portion. It is a steep climb and the road takes a U turn at almost every bend. A narrow foot path allows travelers on foot to cover the distance in a short time but it is tiring. On the way one passes through a small town called Helang. Here the road becomes very narrow and once a bus full of passengers was washed away by flash floods. The last petrol pump on the Badrinath route is 4 km short of Joshimath.

Joshimath, at a height of 1890 m (6000 ft) above sea level is exactly 252 kms from Rishikesh and if everything goes well and there is no unnecessary stoppage enroute due to landslides etc, one can easily reach by a car or a bus in about eleven hours. The locals are called Bhutias and are spread as far as Kumaon. Guru Nanak during his visit to Kumaon had a discussion with Thangar Nath, disciple of Guru Gorakh Nath and won, and the place earlier called Gorakhmata was later on called Nanak Mata which is in the foothills. Locals of Kumaon region celebrate this day with great zeal and serve khichri as prasad. Earlier in the Joshimath region the main occupation of the natives was trading with the Tibetans, but since China has occupied Tibet, this business has stopped. Yak is the main domestic animal of this area. It provides milk to drink, make butter and curd, meat to eat and is used to ploughing fields and carrying luggage. Chaur Sahib (whisker) is made from its white tail, which is used in gurudwaras and temples. Warm clothings are made from its wool and tents are made from its skin. Yak's dung is used for making dung cakes for fuel or converted to organic manure.

Adi Shankaracharya, a statesman, philosopher and a learned man is said to have done tapaysa (penance) under a mulberry tree in a cave in this city. He established the first Matth here and first Dham at Badrinath. Later on four Dhams were established in the four corners of India. He wrote the famous granth called 'Shankar Bhashya' about 1200 years ago besides the commentaries on ten Upanishads. The temple and Matth, where he did tapaysa, is still in good condition and yatris go there to pay their homage. Of special interest is the tree called Kalpavriksh, which is said to be 2400 years old and its circumference is 38 m (120 ft). According to legend, when the Kshir Sagar was churned by Devtas and Demons, 14 Ratans came out and this tree was the first Ratan. All one's wishes are fulfilled if one prays under this tree. In *Guru Granth Sahib*, it is called Parjat. When 14 Ratans were distributed, Inder took this tree to Inderlok and later on as per the wish of Krishna's wife Satbhama, Krishna fought a war with Inder and captured this tree and presented it to his wife. In the *Guru Granth Sahib* there is a mention of it:

Juj meh jor chhali chandrawal
kahan krishan jadam bhaiya
Parjat gopi ley aiyia
brindaban menh rang kiya. 11

(Salok Mahala 1, Asa Di War 13)

Narsingh and Durga temples are the best known of the city's famous temples. In winter when the temple at Badrinath is closed down due to snow, all the deities are brought to NarSingh temple and pilgrims can have darshan here.

Many medicinal plants are found on these mountains. It is believed that, when Lakshman became unconscious in the battle in Sri Lanka, Hanuman brought a piece of hill from this region on which Sanjivini plant grew which cured Lakshman.

It looks strange that men only plough the land while the rest of the work, including harvesting, is done by the women. Potato is a popular crop grown in this area and supplied to the plains. Many kinds of fruits are grown in this area and government has set up fruit preserving factories where jam, squash and other things are prepared and supplied to all parts of India.

Many civil government and Army offices are located in Joshimath. It is a very big trading centre for kasturi, shilajit, honey, woolen shawls, carpets, apples, fruits, etc. which are sent to the plains. While purchasing these things, one should have some knowledge of their purity otherwise there is the risk of being cheated.

It is interesting how the gurudwara in Joshimath came to be built. In 1959, Sardar Shamsher Singh led a jatha to Hemkunt from Kanpur. When they reached Joshimath, they could not get accommodation in any one of the dharamshalas. Perforce they had to spend the night in a verandah of a dharamshala. As luck would have it, it started raining very heavily during the night. They tried to open a room and found one empty, so they settled in it for the rest of the night. In the morning, when the caretaker of the dharamshala came, he was wild and let loose a volley of curses and abuses. They bore them in silence and did not offer explanations or justifications.

Soon after they had left for Gobind Ghat, Havildar Baba Modan Singh, Sant Thandi Singh accompanied by a jatha of thirteen people, and Sant Balwant Singh with four yatris also reached Gobind Ghat. In the evening after the diwan, they discussed the problems faced by the Kanpur jatha. It was decided there and then that a piece of land be purchased in Joshimath and a gurudwara be constructed. The job was entrusted to Sardar Shamsher Singh of Kanpur and Harbhajan Singh of Patna. They went to Joshimath taking Hyat Singh, the professional contractor with them. Hyat Singh offered his own piece of land, but it was not directly connected to the road. While they were debating whether or not to take that land, they happened to pass by a PWD Rest House. They put two and two together, and concluded that sooner or later a road would be built, so they struck a deal and purchased the property for a sum of Rs 4200. They were not far off the mark and the road came up sooner than expected. By the time the Kanpur jatha returned from Hemkunt the land had been bought and preparations to build the gurudwara had begun. Money was collected on the spot and the land was transferred to the Trust's name.

The foundation stone of the gurudwara was laid by five piaras in 1960. It was constructed under the supervision of Sant Thandi Singh. Now this gurudwara is at the centre of the main market. Its Nishan Sahib, though it stands tall, is not visible from a distance as the gurudwara is located at a lower elevation. It is called Gurudwara Dusht Daman and it is a very convenient transit camp for the pilgrims. The big mountain in front of the Gurudwara across Alakhnanda is Hathi Parbat, named so since it resembles an elephant. Its trunk side stretches up to Vishnu Prayag.

There is a gate system from Joshimath to Badrinath for vehicles. The gate opens at six o'clock in the morning and closes at four in the evening. It is closed after every two hours so that vehicles from the opposite direction can pass. A bus takes about an hour to reach Gobind Ghat. There is also a narrow zigzag footpath by which one can reach Vishnu Prayag in half an hour. This is the fifth prayag on this route where the Dhauli Ganga meets Alakhnanda. Gobind Ghat can be reached in one-and-a-half hours on foot from here.

The road from Vishnu Prayag to Gobind Ghat is very narrow with high mountains on either side and the river Alakhnanda flows fast side by side. All along there are lots of waterfalls and the scenic beauty is simply enchanting. Lots

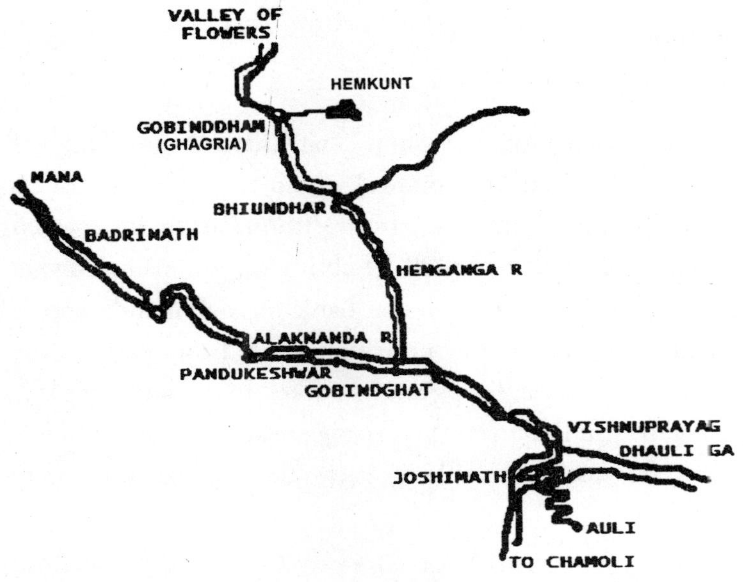

Route from Joshimath to Valley of Flowers and Hemkunt.

of accidents take place in this hazardous section and they are invariably fatal.

On the other side of Joshimath, there is a skiing resort called Auli. It is connected with Joshimath by a ropeway which was constructed in 1992 and is 3.92 km in length and covers the distance in 25 minutes. Prior to 1962 the metalled road existed up to Piplikoti, but after the Indo-China war it was extended by the Border Roads Organisation up to Badrinath and is maintained by them.

Fifth Halt
GOBIND GHAT

The local name of Gobind Ghat is Ghat Chatti (Nanda Singh of Bhiondar village calls it Somtawe), and it is at a distance of 18 km from Joshimath and 10 km from Vishnu Paryag. It is located at a height of 1828 m (5800 ft) above sea level. Gurudwara Gobind Ghat is situated on the bank of Alakhnanda and is approximately one km from the main road. Buses park on the road side whereas cars/jeeps can be parked in the parking place provided by the Trust near the gurudwara at a very nominal fee. Coolies are easily available to carry the luggage up to the dharamshala.

At first sight the market seems very much like Bazaar Mai Sewan in Amritsar. But the market caters for the pilgrims. One can get any item helpful for the journey to Hemkunt like walking sticks with iron spikes, plastic rain coat, good shoes, saropas (scarves tied on the head) and woolens to keep off the cold. The shops also sell souvenirs like photographs and posters of Hemkunt, religious books, audio cassettes, etc. but at double the price as compared to Delhi. People who are not used to hardships and community living normally stay in the small hotels which are comparatively expensive. When accommodation is not available in the gurudwara complex then, as a last resort, one may stay in a hotel.

After passing the market, one can see the beautiful buildings of the gurudwara complex on both sides of the road. Though the gurudwara building is original but with the influx of yatris increasing every year more and more accommodation had to be built. On the left is the main building of the gurudwara. Trust office, langar and accommodation for lodging. On the right there is the accommodation for living, cloak room and the enquiry office where allotment is done. Alakhnanda Ghat, as it is now named, is also on the right hand side where yatris bathe in the running cold water and wash their clothes. The clothes dry easily when the weather is very dry and the boulders on which they are spread for drying get heated under the sun. The latest living rooms have attached bathrooms and latrines and there are also separate common toilets and bathrooms in each block and near the ghats. The suspension bridge that spans the river Alakhnanda is just beyond the gurudwara.

After paying obeisance in the gurudwara, one goes to the office to register, and then accommodation is allotted. If the jatha is large, one should have a typed list of all the members, giving their names, age, gender and address. This procedure is mandatory at every gurudwara. A slip of paper authorizing the person concerned to collect the blankets from the store is given. There is a store in each building. Every room is provided with

Gurudwara Gobind Ghat in 1966

durries, foam mattresses and pillows as well. Before leaving the blankets must be returned to the store after folding them neatly.

There is no dearth of blankets in any gurudwara. Blankets are used/misused daily by different sets of people. Sometimes people have to spread them in the verandah and galleries due to shortage of accommodation. Sometimes blankets get wet also. At the end of the season a contract is awarded for washing/dry-cleaning of the blankets. It is said that an order has been placed for a dry-cleaning plant which will be installed at Gobind Ghat.

Hot tea is served throughout the day but the langar (community kitchen) is open only at set times. Though the management has done its best to construct enough accommodation, sometimes it runs short and yatris are forced to sleep in the verandahs/galleries. There are plans to build more accommodation.

The yatris come from all over India, even from foreign countries. A few hardy people undertake the yatra on foot also from their starting station. It is interesting to watch the mode of transport used by yatris. A majority of yatris travel by buses in organized Jathas. But individual families or small jathas travel by cars/Sumo. It is exhilarating to see people travelling on scooters and bicycles. It is estimated that 1.5 to 2 lakhs people visit Hemkunt in the season which is for four months only (second week of June to first week of October). For the rest of the year it is snowbound.

Vehicles cannot be plied beyond Gobind Ghat. From here, one has to trek the distance. People who cannot undertake the journey on foot can use mules, porters and sedan chairs which are available. Mules start the journey after crossing the suspension bridge. The rates for a mule are negotiable and they depend upon supply and demand and, of course, the weather. If there are more yatris then the rate goes up. It is recommended that the rates should be fixed by the trust or Garhwal Vikas Mandal and licences issued to enforce the rates strictly. Mules are brought from the plains in the season and are also used to ferry construction material and other material. Porters/Kandiwalahs (with a basket at the back) can be hired to carry luggage, children, the aged and sick people. One kandiwallah can carry up to 100 kg of weight. A group of four labourers carry the passenger in the sedan chair supported upon dandies (poles). The movement of all the four persons is completely synchronized, like that of soldiers on parade.

Hem Ganga, which originates from Hemkunt Sarovar and also carries water which flows through the Valley of Flowers, joins the Alakhnanda at Gobind Dham. Prior to building the Hemkunt Gurudwara, Hem Ganga was known as Lakshman Ganga. Pandukeshwar which is one km ahead on Badrinath route can be reached either by mule track or road. Vishnu Mandir is located here and many sadhus come and stay here to do tapasya. Pandu Raja did tapasya at this place, which is mentioned both in *Mahabharat* and *Bachitar Natak*.

Havildar Modan Singh felt that it was not possible for all the yatris to cover the distance from Joshimath to Ghagria (now Gobind Dham) on foot in one day, so they should have a place to stay near Pandukeshwar where they could spend the night. He also felt that there should be a dharamshala and a place which should be open throughout the year, from where he could preach the Sikh religion. He should be able to teach Punjabi to the locals, tell them about gurbani and Sikh history. If possible they should open a small dispensary. He confided in Nanda Singh about his plans as he was a local man. There was a long and circuitous route earlier from the main road to the suspension bridge over Alakhnanda, made of ropes and timber. Havildar Modan Singh gave a contract to Nanda Singh to make a short path through the jungle on payment of Rs 80. While he was constructing the path, his uncle Natha Singh came there and from him he came to know that he had some land in this area. Nanda Singh persuaded him to sell a small piece of land measuring 50'x50'. He informed him that a dharamshala for pilgrims to Hemkunt would be built and he would be taken as caretaker and that he could also open a tea shop. Natha Singh agreed to sell the land and asked for Rs 200. After negotiation he agreed to Rs 150. Nanda Singh went to Pandukeswar and dropped a post card worth three paisa to Havildar Modan Singh in Mussoorie. Havildar Modan Singh on receiving the post card reached Pulna village on 15 March 1943 and met Natha Singh. Next day they went to Tehsil Chamoli where the transfer deed was signed and Havildar Modan Singh returned to Mussorie. Another version is that he obtained two 'Nali' of land from the government and leveled it.

The contract for constructing the dharamshala was awarded to contractor Shri Ganga Singh, who had built the Gurudwara at Hemkunt, for Rs 900 in September 1944. The construction work started in 1944-45. A big hall for the yatris, two rooms with a verandah in front, and a small room for langar were constructed. Havildar Modan Singh named this place as Gobind Ghat after Guru Gobind Singh. Nanda Singh was made in charge and Havildar Modan Singh returned to Mussoorie. Nanda Singh planted lots of fruit trees and made the place a very pleasant one. People visiting Badrinath started stopping here. Even government officials on tour found this place very pleasant and used to stay overnight. Many dignitaries have visited Gobind Ghat including the late President Dr Rajendra Prasad and the late Prime Minister Indira Gandhi while returning from Badrinath. They were all greatly impressed by the arrangements made for the comfort of pilgrims. All tourists going to the Valley of Flowers also stay at Gobind Ghat.

During the yatri season Havildar Modan Singh used to come and spend a lot of time looking after the Hemkunt yatris. He collected money from his friends and relatives, from selling the crops from his own fields in his village, and he used to get money from Rishikesh where people sent their donations. He started langar both at Gobind Ghat and Gobind Dham. The first bag of wheat for the langar was donated by S. Gurmakh Singh of Ludhiana.

The foundation stone of the modern gurudwara was laid in 1949-50 and it was completed by 1955. The cost of the land was Rs 800 and the contract for the plinth was awarded for Rs 80. The contract for the main building was awarded to contractor Dayal Singh Bhandari for Rs 23,000.

In 1967, a jatha consisting of 400 devotees reached here from Kanpur. Piara Singh Kohli, who was a pilgrim, thought that a modern building should be constructed with attached bath rooms for the convenience of the yatris. He appealed to the public and agreed to meet the entire cost himself. Major Teja Singh Samara who was the leader of the group, accepted his proposal and the foundation stone was laid by five piaras. In 1969, when the jatha was coming from Kanpur, a large stone rolled down and hit the bus in which 27 yatris died, two kilometres short of Joshimath. The dead bodies were brought to Gobind Ghat and cremated on the banks of the Alakhnanda. It was decided to build a big hall at that place in memory of the dead. The meeting place of Alakhnanda and Hem Ganga was also named as Gobind Prayag.

Improvement continues. A new building named Dashmesh Bhawan after Guru Gobind Singh is being built on the right hand side of the road. Three floors of the South Block were inaugurated on 7 September 2002. This block will have five floors, each consisting of seven rooms with attached bath rooms. Similarly, construction work of the North Block is also in progress and it is expected that both the buildings will be ready by 2003 before the beginning of the yatra.

Gobind Dham is at a distance of 13 km from Gobind Ghat and it is a progressive climb throughout. The first two kilometres and the last three involve a very steep climb. The journey is very tough for elderly yatris (whether men or women) and for those who have never taken a walk in the plains. This distance should be completed in six hours but some people complete it in nine to ten hours. For those who cannot walk, alternative modes of transport are available. They can hire mules, Kandhiwalas or Dandiwalas.

Before starting, people must deposit their surplus luggage in the cloakroom, which is kept free of charge. Jewellery and cash can also be deposited in the office. Usually there are long queues at the cloakroom so plan accordingly.

The big notice board, on the way leading to the suspension bridge, carries many useful instructions. Read these instructions carefully and act accordingly. These instructions are repeated in the gurudwara at the end of each diwan also. Pay attention to them. The first caution is that if you are suffering from blood pressure, sugar (diabetes), heart problem and asthama, please do not undertake this journey. At the altitude of 15,000 ft, density of oxygen becomes very low, and it could be fatal for people having these diseases. Normally 10 to 15 yatris die in a year while undertaking this yatra. So why take the risk?

The second important instruction relates to the refreshment shops and their rates. These wayside shacks and shops are situated throughout the way. The rates vary according to the altitude and distance. So before purchasing anything always ask for the rate and if it suits your pocket, buy it. Do not get into any arguments. Nearer Hemkunt the prices are approximately four times higher than those in the plains.

The third instruction is not to carry any type of plastic items and polythene sheets with you. Even if you do have them, please do not throw them on the way or at the destination and help save the environment. Plastic items are not biodegradable.

Make sure that you have a good raincoat. One never knows when it will start raining. Plastic raincoats are cheaply available in the market and after completing the journey, one can gift them to someone else for reuse. One should wear comfortable and light walking P.T. shoes. Never walk with new shoes Do not ever walk with leather shoes as they are heavy and can cause blisters, especially if they get wet. Do not be surprised if toenails become blue and separate from the skin below. It happens often and they have to be removed.

Always carry a walking stick with a metal spike at the bottom end. This will help while walking and perhaps prevent you from slipping. Be careful when you have to cross a glacier, especially if you undertake the journey in early June. Glaciers can be very dangerous, as sometimes the upper surface appears to be intact and solid, but underneath it is soft. The sheer weight of a human body makes it give way which can prove to be very dangerous. Never walk alone but do keep some distance from each other. In case of an accident, the other companion can render some help.

Take minimum luggage while undertaking this yatra. Just carry the minimum needs of daily use for two to three days, one change of dress and a pair of surplus socks. It is so cold that clothes do not get dirty. Always carry a big torch, some candles, a match box and some medicines for common ailments.

At Gobind Ghat, Alakhnanda is crossed on a ropeway bridge. Earlier, it was a temporary bridge made of jute ropes and timber. In 1948 the government built a permanent bridge with steel ropes. After the construction of this bridge, the economy of the nearby villages registered an improvement due to easy movement of their produce. After crossing the bridge, the locals believe that they have entered Lokpal territory, which means God's territory, as he is the protector of everyone.

The path is made of stones, of various shapes and sizes embedded in the earth, and is wide enough for two mules to cross. Earlier it was a narrow footpath only. When the Valley of Flowers became famous, a senior forest officer of Uttar Pardesh came to visit it. He asked for Nanda Singh as a guide and also asked him suggest a good location for a rest house. The place suggested by Nanda Singh was accepted and a rest house was built at Ghagria (Gobind Dham). Nanda Singh requested him that a better path should be made and this work was undertaken in 1945.

Often one hears pleas of the muleteers to move so that the mules can pass. Always keep to the mountain side. It is very difficult to walk, and when it rains, it becomes very slippery. Always walk with ease and not in a great hurry. If you get tired or exhausted, rest for a few minutes leaning on the stick while standing, then move again because if you sit for a longer time, your body temperature will drop and it will stiffen and you will find it difficult to maintain the earlier speed. Do not sit down for a long time at the wayside shops. Take a short rest, have a cup of hot tea and then move on. Avoid cold drinks as your body is hot and sweating and with a cold drink one can fall sick.

The first two kilometres are very steep and the path zigzags. If you look downwards you get a panoramic view of Gobind Ghat, its buildings and the flags fluttering near the Gurudwara. One can see Alakhnanda flowing with full fury and Hem Ganga rushing to meet it. When the track levels out there is a check post where the government collects Rs 20 from each mule owner. On an average about 400 to 500 mules cross the post and the money so collected is supposed to be spent on cleaning the area and maintaining it, but it is hardly done as one can see plastic bags all over the place. After this post the track follows Hem Ganga on the right hand side and the the sound of rushing water is music to the ears. Enjoying the mountains and breathing fresh air one moves forward slowly and steadily. Everyone keeps on chanting and reciting Satnam Wahe Guru. If one keeps on remembering Guru Gobind Singh and the Almighty God the journey becomes easier and it is his responsibility to take you up for darshan. It may be a myth or a reality but faith definitely helps. Reciting gurbani hymns with every step makes the journey easier. The writing of Guru Arjun Dev Ji and Bhai Gurdas ji suggest that:

Charan Chalo marg Gobind
Mitey pap japiye har bind (Sukhmani Mahla 5, page 218)
Charan saran gur ek painda jaye chal
Satgur kot painda aage hoy laet hai (Kabit Bhai Gurdas Ji)

When the yatris get tired, they chant the following and somehow get renewed energy:

Wah wah Gobind Singh ji
Hemkunt wasi Guru Gobind Singh ji
Kalgi wale Guru Gobind Singh ji
Darshan deo Guru Gobind Singh ji
Phera pao Guru Gobind Singh ji

Khadi udikan Guru Gobind Singh ji
Chheti aao Guru Gobind Singh ji
Amrit de datey Guru Gobind Singh ji
Sarbans dani Guru Gobind Singh ji
Anand pur wasi Guru Gobind Singh ji
Hemkunt wasi Guru Gobind Singh ji.

Whenever the yatris meet, they always greet each other with Wahe Guru ji ka Khalsa , Wahe Guru ji ki Fateh. Yatris coming down should always encourage the yatris who are going up. This will put them in high spirits and vigour. It is seen that people distribute dry fruits, glucose powder, sweets, etc. This brings about a feeling of togetherness and friendship among strangers.

Just about three kilometres from Gobind Ghat is the village Pulna. This village is also owned by the villagers of Bhiondar. In winter they move down to Pulna and in summer they go up to Bhiondar. There are lots of tea shops on the way where one can have a short break if desired. From here it is more or less level walking requiring less effort. At a distance of eight kilometers one comes across the important village named Bhiondar. The yatris gets the first view of the snow capped mountains at a distance from here. This village has played a very important and vital role since 1934 and specially in carrying the yatris to Hemkunt literally by holding them by hand upto 1953. Bhai Nanda Singh belongs to this very village and he has been associated throughout with this holy cause in the company of God fearing personalities like Sant Sohan Singh, Havildar Modan Singh and Sant Thandi Singh. He is an old man now, yet his memory is excellent and he can recall all the events from 1934 to this day very clearly.

From this village, for two kilometres, the walk is very smooth and one can walk comfortably. Then one crosses the Hem Ganga, over a wooden bridge. From here, with the river flowing on the left, the difficult climb starts. It is very steep and one has to rest after a short distance. In early June one comes across a glacier before the wooden bridge. All around there is dense forest and pin drop silence. One cannot even hear the chirping of birds or see the river or hear its roar. There is no life here and it looks like this is the end of the world. One can see yatris taking brief halts as they criss cross each other. Though it is cold one tends to perspire due to exertion. This can lead to dehydration. So keep sipping small amounts of glucose or salty water. It is not advisable to take a long rest, but keep on moving slowly. Through the forest and stiff climb the path leads to the high open meadow that blooms with rare mountain flowers. At some distance one can see a helipad, where VIPs land by helicopter either to visit Hemkunt or the Valley of Flowers. There is a small meteorological office where rain fall and other data are collected and sent to the main office.

Though the distance to Gobind Dham is only 750 m from the helipad, it seems it will never come an end. On the way one comes across a small forest rest house and a small hospital. Then one can see mules and the beginning of the market. Everyone thanks God that the first day's arduous climb and journey is over as one reaches Gobind Dham. After crossing the market one sees the Nishan Sahib of the Gurudwara.

On the way, I asked a lot of yatris why they undertook this tough yatra. Some people answered that they wanted to visit the holy place where Guru Gobind Singh did tough tapaysa in his previous birth. There aim was clear: to reach Hemkunt as early as possible, take a dip in the sarovar, pay homage, collect the prasad and amrit (holy water) and return as early as possible. Some yatris said that they had prayed to get their wishes fulfilled and were going there for thanksgiving and to pay homage. One yatri said that he had been ordered by Guru Gobind Singh in his dream to visit. Some of them come because their friends and relatives were coming to pay the visit, and there were extra seats in the bus/car so they thought it best that they too take the opportunity to go on a pilgrimage. Only a few said they had come on an excursion or to enjoy nature.

I think that in a short period of four months, the number of people who undertake this journey must be a record for any pilgrimage centre. I wonder whether there is any pilgrimage centre at such a height (except in Tibet). When I went on the Kailash Mansarovar yatra, I did not see any building though we crossed Dolma Pass at a height of 19,200 feet (please see my book *Kailash Mansrovar – Thirty days of adventure and ecstasy*). The journey to Hemkunt at this time echoes with the name of Satnam Wahe Guru, Jo Bole So Nihal – Sat Sri Akal and Wahe Guru ji ka Khalsa and Wahe Guru ji ki Fateh.

The Last Halt
GOBIND DHAM

Starting from Gobind Ghat early in the morning, one can easily reach Gobind Dham in the afternoon. Though one is badly tired but the spirits are high as one is nearing the destination. This place was earlier called Ghagria. When the locals used to visit Lokpal for puja , they used to change their dress and wear simple clothes. The ladies used to leave behind their ghagries (long petticoats) here, so the name became popular. When Guru Gobind Singh's 300th birth anniversary was being celebrated, the Sangat unanimously passed a resolution changing its name to Gobind Dham (Abode of Gobind), though in official (revenue) records it is still called Ghagria. It is situated at a height of 3048 m (10,500 ft) above sea level. It is here that both the pilgrims and trekkers halt for the final ascent to Hemkunt and the Valley of Flowers. Though a lot of accommodation was built recently, it is still very difficult to find a place for sleeping at night. The reason is simple; most of the yatris have to stay here for two nights, once while going up to Hemkunt and again after returning. If one can manage to return after visiting Hemkunt by 2 o'clock in the afternoon, then it is advisable to go straight to Gobind Ghat but it is not easy for everyone. On reaching here one gets a cup of hot tea and langar is served throughout the day as there is a constant flow of yatris from both direction – Gobind Ghat and Hemkunt.

Gobind Dham is very quiet and pleasant. Being at a height and with the gentle breeze blowing, one gets refreshed. It is surrounded by high mountains and Hem Ganga and other streams flow nearby. The place becomes active and busy between the months of June and October; the rest of the year it is snowbound and inaccessible. It has a shopping cum marketing centre besides the tourist and forest rest house. Every year the number of shops and hotels increases to cater to the needs of the growing number of pilgrims and tourists. The shops sell necessities for the journey ahead and a wide variety of souvenirs. The prices are obviously higher than in Gobind Ghat. The market becomes deserted when the pilgrims move up/down. After crossing the market, the gurudwara is located on the left side.

Hemkunt Gurudwara was first constructed in 1936 and very few people knew about it so there were only casual visitors to

Gurudwara Gobind Dham in 1966

this place. Bhiondar village was a night stop from where they started the journey early in the morning. It was very difficult to make the round trip in a day. Since there was no shelter Havildar Modan Singh and Sant Thandi Singh used to rest and spend the night in the hollow of a tree trunk. This famous tree still exists. It is located near gate number 2 and has been accorded a prominent status. In 1942, Havildar Modan Singh decided to build a dharamshala at Ghagria, so that the pilgrims could halt at night. The contract to build the dharamshala was awarded to Nanda Singh for Rs 400. This was completed within the same year and became famous as Ghagria Dharamshala.

In 1962, the foundation stone of a bigger gurudwara was laid and by June 1964 this gurudwara became a reality under the supervision of Sant Thandi Singh. When a jatha visited this place in June 1964, a very interesting event took place which is narrated in a book called *Shri Hemkunt Sahib Dian Pawan Yatra* (published by Chief Khalsa Diwan, Kanpur). It narrates that "A ball of dazzling light traveled from the door and after paying homage to the Guru Granth Sahib, went back without causing any damage or hurting anybody. The light was of such high intensity that all those who were praying with eyes closed were dazzled. At once Jo Bole so Nihal – Sat Sri Akal, the traditional jaikara (word of praise) by the Sikhs, was chanted and relayed again and again and devotees started saying 'Wahe Wahe Guru Gobind Singh ji'. When S. Daljit Singh and his colleagues who

Another view of the Gurudwara

were preparing langar, heard this they rushed to the gurudwara. When they came to know about the incident, they started crying, as they were in the langar so they could not witness such an incident. What was their fault, they grieved. Wahe Guru heard this plea and the same incident took place a second time. A streak of lightning came again, paid respects to Guru Granth Sahib and went out from the same door. Some people thought that it might have been due to bad weather outside and lightning striking the Gurudwara. When they went outside, they found that the sky was all clear with twinkling stars. They all were convinced that it was a 'chamatkar' (miracle) by Wahe Guru and everyone bowed in reverence."

Considering the need, new buildings for more and more accommodation are coming up. A building donated by Kenya Sangat (South Africa) was inaugurated in 1988 and a foundation stone for an other building was laid. This is an ongoing work. It is hoped that in times to come, all the yatris can stay at this place comfortably. Along with Hemkunt, Gobind Dham was among the first place at such an altitude to be surveyed by Survey of India.

It was decided that Sant Thandi Singh would stay at Gobind Dham whereas Havildar Modan Singh would look after Gobind Ghat. Each was desirous that Nanda Singh should stay with him but it was later decided that Nanda Singh would stay at Gobind Dham with Sant Thandi Singh.

Aukhi ghati yatra bhi aukhi te bikhra penda
Ang sang tu satguru mere aukhey wele sahara tenda 11

> Hey Wahe Guru, next journey which I am to under take is very difficult as the route is very tough. Please help me in all respects, and without your assistance I cannot undertake this journey.

The last journey, though it is only five kilometres long one has to gain about five thousand feet starting from 10,100 feet and ultimately reaching 15,210 feet. For every metre, one gains the height of one foot, and to reach Hemkunt 50,000 steps of a height of six inches have to be taken. No doubt it is a very difficult climb. The best thing is to get up as early as possible and after finishing the morning rituals, perform the ardas and start walking in the cool morning breeze. The object should be to reach Hemkunt as early as possible, so that one can return in time, as normally the weather deteriorates in the afternoon and nobody is allowed to spend the night there.

The pilgrims start the journey in biting cold weather and even a drizzle. After crossing a wooden bridge on Hem Ganga, the journey starts in earnest. The first half kilometre is a modest climb, then the tough climb starts and goes up to the end. There is no problem for the young, army men and locals, but for the others it is a nightmare. It is the magnetic pull of Hemkunt and in spite of all the difficulties one keeps on moving. Dusht Daman seems to be calling you and inspiring you to keep on moving. If one finds it difficult to walk, then it is advisable to take the services of a mule or a coolie. If one has not been able to traverse the distance from Gobind Ghat to Gobind Dham in seven hours, then one should take some assistance to reach Hemkunt Sahib.

On the way, groups of tea stalls are to be found with temporary structures made from local material and roofed with plastic sheets. The yatris can rest there for a short time and take a refreshing hot drink. There are long benches where one can even stretch one's legs. In 1966, there was only one tea stall near Bhiondar village where tea and hot pakoras were served but now one will find a tea stall at every step of the journey selling all sorts of drinks but at three to four times the price in the plains.

From here one gets a clear view of snow covered mountain peaks for the first time. It is odd to see a house at such a height and people from the plains always wonder how local people reach there and what they do for their living. Fog plays hide and seek with nature. If it is raining the path becomes wet and slippery and one has to be extra careful. In the beginning only some trees and bushes are seen. Thereafter one will find jungles of Bhoj Patra trees. The local people use the outer skin (rough layer) of the tree for roofing the huts. The inner layers, called Bhoj Patra, were used as paper in earlier days. Old granths written on these Bhoj Patras are found in museums and elsewhere. The government awards contracts to the local people for removing the "skin" from the trunks every year and if any one attempts to remove it unauthorizedly, it is considered theft and is punishable.

While walking, if one looks up, one finds yatris walking at the higher reaches. One gets frightened at the thought of how to climb to such a height. But if one keeps on moving at a steady pace with the goal in view and with the help of Wahe Guru, one will reach the destination. After covering half the distance, it becomes difficult to breathe, which means there is less oxygen in the atmosphere as there are no trees. With the lack of oxygen it is strenuous to walk, the body becomes heavy, a feeling of nausea and pain in the heart region occurs. If you experience any of these symptoms then you should sit down, take a long deep breath, and only when the body recovers, proceed further. Take the assistance of the nearby yatri, and if you still feel unwell, then climb down. Normally after taking a few steps downwards one should feel well. Hire a mule at this stage, they are available on the route, even though they will charge more.

For one kilometre after the jungle finishes lots of Brahm kamals are to be found. People get surprised to see the lotuses growing in the mountain area as they usually grow in water only. The flowers are merely shaped like lotus flowers hence they are called Brahm kamal. It is better not to touch or smell the flower. Do not pluck or throw it away. Outside it is covered with layers of covering and inside there is a blue coloured flower. There is an interesting tale in Mahabharat about this flower. During the banvas (sojourn) of the Pandavas, their consort, Draupadi saw this flower floating in Alakhnanda and asked Bhim to get one for her. He could not find it growing anywhere nearby and went searching for it. Further up, on the way to Badrinath, he found an old monkey sleeping across the path. The monkey's tail was sprawled on the path and was an obstruction. Bhim said, 'O monkey, remove your tail so that I can proceed on my mission.' The monkey replied, 'I am a very old monkey and am helpless. So please assist me in moving away my tail and keeping it somewhere else.' It is said that the powerful Bhim, who threw the elephants in space which are said to be still revolving, could not move the tail in spite of all his might. Realizing the monkey as a mightier being he apologized and asked for his identity. The monkey replied that he was Ram Bhagat, Hanuman. Bhim requested him to appear in his real form. Bhim had the darshan of Hanuman and asked him where he could find Brahm kamal flowers. He pointed towards Hemkunt. Now there is a temple at this place, Hanuman Chatti, where people pray, especially the drivers, for a safe journey.

In early June, one may encounter a glacier for a considerable distance while nearing the end of the journey near the stairway. Though all precautions are taken by fixing ropes etc. one has to be very careful and take each step carefully. Never walk in a hurry or in a heedless manner. It is best to step into the footprints of earlier travellers. One wrong step can send you down the gorge and prove fatal. The yatris on mules also have to get down because the mules cannot walk on snow. From a distance the Nishan Sahib is sighted at last. But there is still a long way to go. From here the path divides. One is made up of steps and the other is the lengthy mule track. In June when it is covered with snow, only the steps route can be taken. The steps themselves are cleared of snow, though the snow is heaped on the sides. Nature takes its own time to melt the snow on the mule path. It is often washed away by the rains.

HEMKUNT SAHIB

Hemkunt Sahib, as described in *Bachitar Natak*, is the place where Guru Gobind Singh, also known as Dusht Daman, the destroyer of enemies, had done deep meditation in his previous birth for a long time. God was pleased with him and he transcended duality. He had become one with the Almighty and his creation. Not willing to leave that state of consciousness, he was content being there. But God instructed him to take one more birth to complete the work started by Guru Nanak. So he was born as Gobind Das in the home of GuruTegh Bahadur, the ninth Guru carrying the torch of Guru Nanak.

With the passage of time, and the enterprising spirit of some individuals, a small gurudwara was constructed which later on, when more and more devotees started visiting, took the shape of a modern gurudwara.

After climbing 1175 steps (or taking a longer route) when a devotee sees the flutering saffron Nishan Sahib, he stops at the last step, either to relax or thank God (Wahe Guru) that he has achieved what he had been dreaming of. His eyes open wide in wonder when he sees the magnificent gurudwara at such a height. Only Sikhs can do such things, whereas other may think them impossible.

The path that the yatris have just left behind was constructed in 1953, at a cost of Rs 5000 only and no changes have been made on this route. Millions of pilgrims have reached their destination using this route without any difficulty. Yatris thank Baba Modan Singh for his far-sightedness in getting this path built.

It is surprising that there is no mention of Hemkunt in his life as Guru Gobind Singh. Historians have not been able to establish whether he visited this place. The only reference to it comes in *Bachitar Natak* and that of his previous birth. But that was enough inspiration for some devoted Sikhs to locate the place, even though the search was long and tedious. And then it inspired others to build a magnificent gurudwara at such a height. Since then there is a never ending flow of pilgrims to Hemkunt Sahib between the months of June to October.

The gurudwara is situated on a level ground with a lake in front and is surrounded by mountains on three sides. It stands 4320 m, (15,200) ft above sea level. It is a double-storeyed building occupying 13,000 sq ft of land. The building is designed in the shape of a butterfly.

Though most of the Sikh gurudwaras have sarovars built around them, here the gurudwara is built on the bank of the sarovar, the lake measuring 400 m in length and 300 m in width approximately. On three sides of this lake stand tall and mighty mountains called Sapt Sring, the seven peaks.

As per the traditions, before entering a gurudwara one must take a holy dip in the sarovar. Facing the gurudwara, on the right hand side, a shed has been constructed for men to change clothes and take a dip in the holy lake. For ladies a separate bathing place has been made in the gurudwara, so that they can take a dip in privacy. The water from the lake is so canalized that it flows to the gurudwara. The icy waters originating from a glaciers seem daunting but the holy bath refreshes one, not just physically but spiritually also. Since the water is icy cold it is hard to take the second dip. The aim is fulfilled as the Gurus have said:

Kar ishnan simar parbhu apna

Man tan bheae aroga 11

Take a bath and remember God.

It will keep your mind and body healthy.

After the long and arduous climb, the yatris are too tired to go for a bath but everyone advises them to do so. And surprisingly, the moment they touch the cold water, their fatigue disappears magically. Many yatris stay in the water long enough to recite the first five pauris of Japji. But when they come out of the water, their condition is pathetic. Since the blood temperature comes down due to cold water, a longer stay in the water can prove harmful. But no one can forget God while taking a dip, and that is the motive underlying it. A dip in the holy sarovar ought to cleanse not just the body but also the mind of all its vices. Many people with incurable diseases have come here and gone back in a healthier state. Whether it is the power of faith or the healing power of the lake that does wonders is a subject that can never be settled one way or the other. Like the chicken-and-egg or the seed-and-tree controversy. No one can say which came before the other. Similarly no one can say with authority what healed their ailing bodies, but many have felt better after a bath in Hemkunt.

After a bath, some yatris change into new clothes thinking they have become clean and pious. Considering the water from the lake to be holy, many people fill their plastic bottles with it terming it as amrit (nectar). They keep this bottled water near the *Granth Sahib* and after Ardas take it home where it is distributed as prasad among friends and relatives.

The circumference of the lake is approximately two kilometres. But there is no pathway around it. There are many streams flowing from Sapt Sring. Between the fourth and fifth stream there is a small lake and when it overflows the water falls into the main lake, Hemkunt. All the streams and lakes are frozen in winter. Some yatris undertake to go round the lake and it takes them two hours to do so since there is no trodden path there. Most pilgrims are too tired after the steep climb and do not undertake this challenge.

The overflow of the lake takes the form of a stream named Hem Ganga. Another stream flowing from the Valley of Flowers joins it and makes it a river. At Gobind Ghat it meets Alakhnanda which is full of fun and frolic. A small turbine has been installed on the outflow of the river from the lake. It generates electricty for the gurudwara.

The seven peaks, which were refered to in *Bachitar Natak*, are Ghori Parbat at a height of 23,000 ft; Hathi Parbat; Vishisht Parbat; Kapeen Parbat; Kar Parbat; and the sixth and seventh are smaller peaks with no names.

It snows heavily in winter. It is recorded that about forty feet of snow falls every winter. Sometimes the entire building, and even the Nishan Sahib, gets covered in snow. The snow hardens and acts like a beam taking the full load. The snow does not melt with the sun but gets washed away by the rain. In 1964, the previous gurudwara and the Nishan Sahib got completely buried in the snow. It could not be located. Help of Hyat Singh, the contractor was sought. He came with his force of workers and with sheer imagination started digging a tunnel through the snow. The tunnel was large enough to allow a man to crawl through it. After digging for 20 to 25 feet they reached the gurudwara and managed to open the lock.

A hot cup of tea awaits the pilgrims at all hours. After the bath they head straight for it, and get warmed up in no time. Nothing tastes better than that hot cup of tea served with love in stainless steel tumblers. Maybe it is just the thing wanted at that time. Langar of khichri is served subsequently. Refreshed and fortified, the yatris climb to the darbar hall of the gurudwara to pray to the Guru Granth Sahib. Offerings are made in the form of money, ornaments, ingredients for langar and romallas (a set of four piece cloth to cover the Granth Sahib). It is seen that there is an abundance of romallas and they have to be sent down as there is not enough storage space up there in Hemkunt. If the yatris brought blankets instead of romallas they could be put to better use by the management.

Ardas (a formal prayer of the Sikhs) is performed twice a day, at 10 o'clock in the morning and at 1o'clock in the afternoon. The granthi narrates the significance of the place as described in *Bachitar Natak*. It is punctuated with loud cries of jaikara (Bole

A view of the Gurudwara with the frozen lake.

so Nihal – Sat Sri Akal) The echo is heard in the entire valley. Then Karah Prashad is distributed to the congregation.

It is best to start the return journey immediately after the second ardas, as it is observed that the weather turns hostile in the afternoon. There is usually a rainstorm accompanied by cold and strong winds.

On a clear day the pilgrims stand by the side of the lake and try to locate the seven peaks (Sapt Sring) marked by the Nishan Sahibs. They can be seen clearly with the help of binoculars. Sevadars in the gurudwara enchant the audience with spectacular stories of celestial sounds and sights that have been heard and seen. The pilgrims are undoubtedly enthralled by the beauty of the place and listen to them with wide-eyed wonder. Anything and everything seems to be possible in such an enchanting place.

Nobody is allowed to spend the night at Hemkunt because it gets very cold at night. Moreover the rarefied atmosphere makes breathing difficult. Only the sevadars, the servants of the Lord, can stay because they get acclimatised to the atmosphere. But even they are transferred after a short duration. But once you get used to the place you can reach the highest peak of Sapt Sring. These peaks are very high and there are no built up paths. Yet the brave Sikhs, with no training, faced all the hazards on the way and finally succeeded in putting up the Nishan Sahib on all the seven peaks. The names of these Sikhs are Surat Singh and Nanda Singh. Now a team of young and energetic persons from Talwandi sabo, Bhatinda, visit this place in August every year to carry out the repairs, if any, and to change the chola (the saffron cloth wrapped around the pole). Other youngsters are also coming forward to scale these lofty peaks, and perform the same service.

Except for Brahm kamal, no other flower grows at this place. But the Brahm kamal makes up for all others, growing anywhere and everywhere, from the rocks and stones. It is said that those who dared to spend the night in Hemkunt heard strange sounds. Dr Tara Singh of Nahan is said to have spent two months but he has made no mention of any strange sounds in his book. The locals thought he had died and was buried in the snow and were shocked to see him walking back one day.

The climb down is much more difficult, but the yatris seem to be rolling down the hills with a rejuvenated energy. However, one must be careful at each step as it is slippery and wet. It often begins to rain when it is time for them to make the return journey. The descent puts a lot of pressure on the knees and toes and the legs become stiff like logs by the time you reach Gobind Ghat. A massage and crepe bandage can help and yatris should carry a bottle of Iodex and a crepe bandage with them. Some people lose their nails and that takes a long time to heal.

There are people who make the round trip in one day. I met Mata Gurdip Kaur who visited Hemkunt Sahib in 1959 for the first time. Subsequently she has been going there every year, sometimes more than once in a season. I met her in 2002, she was 92 years old, or young, and very active, careful and never walks in a hurry.

Hemkunt Sahib is also known as Lok Pal or Loh Paleshwar by the locals. Lakshman mandir and a dharamshala are situated near the gurudwara where some yatris go and pay their respects. The temple has got two deities – Mahakal and Mahakali. Locals consider this as a very sacred place and come here three times in a year – in October (Bhadron ki Sangrand), Janam Asthmi and Nanda Asthmi. They come bare foot all the way from Ghagria (Gobind Dham) and make sure that they do not have anything made out of leather on them, such as shoes, belt and purse, etc. They even discard the umbrella as on the outer upper part a leather washer is provided so that water does not leak in. They shun intoxicating items, such as liquor or cigarettes. They take a dip in the holy lake and after doing puja, they distribute Karah Prasad (which they cook at home and carry with them). They consider Lok Pal more sacred than Badrinath. It is believed that Devtas come to take a bath in the lake at midnight singing and chanting mantras but no one has ever seen it. People pray for begetting sons and if they come with real devotion, then they are always blessed with one. It is difficult to say how far it is true but undoubtedly faith can work wonders.

Ab main apni katha bakhaano
Tap sadhat jih bidh mohe aano.
Hemkunt Parbat hai jahaṇ
Sapt Sring sohbat hai tahan.

Sapt Sring teh naam kahawa
Panduraj jeh jog kamawa
Teh hum adhik tapasya sadhi
Mahakal Kalika aradhi.

Eh bidh kar tapasya bhayo
Dwai teh ek roop hoye gayo
Taat maat mur alakh aradha
Boh bidh jog sadhna sadha.

Tim jo kari alakh ki seva
Ta te bhaye prasan gurdeva
Tin prabh jab aahis mohe diya
Tab hum janam kalu mein liya.

Chit na bhayo hamra aavan kah
Chubhi rahi surat prabh charanan manh
Jion tion prabh hum ko samjhayo
Iim kahe ke eh lok pathayo.

Bachitar Natak, Dasam Granth

now i will tell my tale

Ab Main Apni Katha Bakhano

Now I will tell you my story
As it was revealed to me in meditation.
Far away in the upper reaches of the Himalayas
Stands the Hemkunt Mountain
Amidst the Seven Peaks of Sapt Sring.

Sapt Sring earned its name because
Panduraj did tapasya in this place
Here I too went into deep meditation
And contemplated on Mahakal and Kalika.

My meditation bore fruit
Duality dissolved into unity with God
My parents, too, engrossed in His remembrance
Prayed and worshipped in many ways.
When their tapasya bore fruit
And the Almighty was pleased with them,
Then I was born to them
And I took birth in this age of Kaliyug.

I was not willing to come again
As my heart was resting at His feet.
Somehow the Almighty Lord persuaded me
And sent me to this world of men and women.

This verse appears in the sixth chapter of *Bachitar Natak*, (The Extraordinary Drama), which is part of *Dasam Granth*, said to be the compilation of all the works of Guru Gobind Singh, the tenth guru of the Sikhs. This verse is sung in every gurudwara in the months of December and January, before and after the tenth master's birth anniversary. Gurpurab. It is this verse that led many a Sikh to traverse the unknown paths and scale daunting heights of the Himalayas to locate the spot mentioned by their guru. Yet, not long ago, this was also the subject of many controversies among the Sikhs.

One of them was concerning the authorship of the *Dasam Granth* itself; whether the *Dasam Granth* was written by Guru Gobind Singh himself or it is a compilation of the works of many poets of his time. And the other controversy dwelt on the authenticity of the volume; which one was the original work of Guru Gobind Singh. Since there are many hand-written books it is not easy to ascertain which one of them is the original granth composed by the Guru.

It is important to dive into history, or whatever is available of it, to come to understand the importance of Hemkunt Sahib, the reference in the *Bachitar Natak* of *Dasam Granth*, and the controversies that ensued and still continue among the Sikhs. It is mentioned in the Adi Purana, chapter 119, Salokas 47 to 50 of the *Mahabharat* that a famous king, Pandu Raja renounced the material world and went into the Himalayas to do tapasya. According to the verse quoted here, Guru Gobind Singh validates the truth of the statement that Pandu Raja also did tapasya in the same place.

From the *Encyclopedia of Sikhism*, it is learnt that Guru

Gobind Singh visited Nahan at the request of Raja Medni Prakash of Nahan. He was taken around the beautiful hill state spreading up to the banks of Yamuna River. The Guru liked the place and decided to stay there. Later it was named Paonta, meaning where the Guru put his foot. Now it is a busy township and is considered a holy place by the Sikhs. Pilgrims on the way to Hemkunt Sahib make it a point to go via Paonta Sahib.

Guru Gobind Singh was a poet, par excellence. He not only composed poetry in many languages himself, but encouraged poets of all languages by giving them a place in his court and presenting rich awards to them. He himself composed poetry in Gurmukhi, Braj Bhasha, Persian and Urdu. Some of his works form the daily prayers of the Sikhs such as Jaap Sahib, Akal Ustat and 33 Swayyas.

The Guru was keen to educate the Sikhs and pull them out of the darkness of ignorance and liberate them from unnecessary burdens of blind superstitions. But most of the religious texts were in Sanskrit and therefore out of the reach of the common man. In those days the Shudras were not even allowed to listen to the recitation of the scriptures. Molten lead was poured into the ears of any person from the lower castes if he by chance happened to listen to the scriptures being read by the haughty brahmins. Naturally the scriptures became the monopoly of the brahmins who exploited the public for vested interests.

Once Guru Gobind Singh called Pandit Raghunath Dass, a brahmin, and asked him to educate the Sikhs in Sanskrit language, at a handsome salary. The proud brahmin said that the Sikhs belonged to the lower castes and were not even entitled to listen to Sanskrit, so the question of teaching them the language did not arise. The Guru took it up as a challenge to educate them. He is said to have selected five intelligent persons, and attiring them in brahmin clothes, he sent them to Kashi in 1742 Bikrami (1685 A.D.) to learn Sanskrit. These persons were Bhai Ganda Singh, Bhai Vir Singh, Bhai Sain Singh, Bhai Karam Singh and Bhai Ram Singh (*Dasam Gur Chamatkar,* p169). He further instructed them to persuade a few brahmin scholars to accompany them on their return after completing their studies. He promised to give them rich rewards. When they returned alongwith many brahmin scholars they were assigned the task of translating the Hindu scriptures into the common language spoken by the people at that time.

That is the reason why most of the works of that period are in the Braj Bhasha, the language commonly spoken at that time. That is also the reason why most of the works are in poetry, because people were not literate and could not write them down. They would sing these verses and pass them on from generation to generation. It is far easier to learn poetry by heart. The other commonly followed tradition among poets of that time was to keep their identity undisclosed. They often wrote in the name of their masters as is evident from the composition of the *Guru Granth Sahib*. Even though it contains the works of six gurus, the first five and the ninth guru, yet each shabad ends in the name of Nanak. Often poets used psuedonyms and also did not disclose the time and place of their compositions. Guru Gobind Singh and the poets of his time followed the same tradition, and that is the reason why there is a controversy regarding the authorship of the *Dasam Granth*. In Ram Avatar, Krishan Avatar and Pakhian Chartar writings, names such as Ram and Shyam were used. And it is said that Guru Gobind Singh and the poets used the same poetic names as nom-de-plumes. That explains the controversy about the authorship of *Dasam Granth*.

At the time of Guru Gobind Singh no book known as *Dasam Granth* existed. It was obviously compiled much later. There is no doubt that the guru wrote copiously. Many believe that the granth called *Vidyasagar* or *Vidyadhar* contained all his works. It is said to have weighed nine maunds, approximately 340 kilograms. It was hand written. In 1704, when Guru Gobind Singh had to cross the flooded river, Sirsa, near Ropar it got washed away. Others believe that it was destroyed in the aftermath of one of the battles. Again not everyone believes that the granth contained the writings of the guru alone. At one point of time there were as many as 52 poets in his darbar. Many think that most of the translations of Hindu scriptures done by the poets of his darbar formed the bulk of the granth. But they all seem to agree that the name of the granth was given by the guru himself.

Giani Gyan Singh, a well-known author of many books on Sikhism, transcribed in Punjabi the *Gurpartap Suraj Prakash Granth* written by Maha kavi Bhai Santokh Singh in poetry, in two volumes known as *Panth Prakash* and *Twareekh Guru Khalsa*. The original was in Braj Bhasha and contained the history of the Sikh Gurus. The former was republished by the Punjabi Language Department of the Punjab Government, Patiala in 1987.

Giani Gyan Singh narrates the story of the *Dasam Granth* in his book titled *Panth Prakash*. He says that the granth was not bound in one volume to begin with. The baanis or hymns suggest that they appeared in different pothis (volumes). Once the Sikhs requested Guru Gobind Singh to put them all together in one granth like the Adi Granth. To this the Guru replied thus, "Guru Arjan was a very pious man and he need not be equalled, either by me or by any of you. The holy granth is to be worshipped like a guru and should remain supreme. It is written in devotion and contains the wisdom of our great gurus and great Hindu and Sufi saints. I have simply translated the Sanskrit granths into the language of the common man." Giani Gyan Singh, *Panth Prakash*, p 320.)

He continues, "Then a day came when, Bhai Mani Singh obtained the permission of the Panth and collected all the baanis of the tenth guru and bound them in one volume (p 320)." The reading of the granth ends with stories (*hakayates*).

The second volume came into being at Dam Dama and was written by Baba Deep Singh, the great martyr. He undertook this work in the year 1804 Samat. The reading of this volume ends with Photik Kabits, Photik Couplets. Some scholars recognize it because of these couplets. Sukha Singh Granthi compiled another volume of the granth at Patna in the year 1832 and included Sukhmana and Chhakey as also some matters of his own choice. The reading of this granth ends with Chhakas.

In this way three different volumes of the granth came into existence. After some time his son, Charat Singh, added four more pages to it, which resembled the handwriting of Guru Gobind Singh and wrote the whole granth again. This volume was purchased by Bawa Hakim Singh and is now placed in the Moti Bagh Gurudwara in Patiala. He made many more copies of the same in his own handwriting. He professed that the four pages of the copies of the granth were written by the guru himself. Thus he managed to charge an exorbitant price for the granths. In this way the three most popular versions of the Dasam Granth came into being." (*Panth Prakash,* pp 321-322)

On the other hand Bhai Kesar Singh Chhibber writes in 'Bansawali Nama, Dasan Padshaiyan Da' that *Dasam Granth* existed in the time of Guru Gobind Singh, which was known as Chhotta Granth, and was placed beside *Guru Granth Sahib*. Before the tenth guru left his mortal frame, he enjoined his Sikhs to follow only *Guru Granth Sahib*, and told them that from then onwards the *Granth Sahib* was their only guru: '*Sab Sikhon ko hukam hai guru manyo granth*.' Thereby he overruled any possibility of another living guru and at the same time denying to any other book the status of *Guru Granth Sahib*. Bhai Kesar Singh Chhibber has quoted the conversation between the guru and his Sikhs stating that the smaller book took birth in the house of the tenth master, and the Sikhs beseeched their master to include it in the Adi Granth as all the earlier gurus had done. To this the master replied that the Adi Granth is the Guru, final and complete. He refused to include his contributions to the Granth.

This was the master's enigmatic game. Who knows the secret why he did not wish to include his compositions in the *Granth Sahib*. He marvels at the mystery of the guru's ways and says, 'All through the ages this question will be asked and no one will be able to give a convincing reply.'

In 1778 Samat Bikrami, Bhai Mani Singh was appointed the head granthi of Darbar Sahib, Amritsar. He dedicated his life to the service of the gurudwara and the Sikhs and earned the goodwill of all, the high and the low. He wrote many religious books and in addition made out a fourth version of *Granth Sahib*, which included the bani of all the gurus as is given in the *Guru Granth Sahib*, but separated it from the Bhaktas' bani. And instead of the compilation on the basis of ragas, he compiled it on the basis of individual guru's bani. In this volume he also included the spritual bani of Guru Gobind Singh as also some of the translations from the Sanskrit texts, and named it *Dasam Padshah ka Granth*.

This version of the Granth attracted the wrath of the Panth, because it is considered sacrilege to edit or make changes in the *Guru Granth Sahib*. Guru Har Rai, the seventh guru, had not spared his son for making a slight variation in one of the shabads. Naturally the Sikhs were not going to spare Bhai Mani Singh even though he had obtained permission of Mata Sundri to write his book. He was martyred in Lahore in 1794 Samat Bikrami. After his death, *Dasam Granth* was sent to Dam Dama Sahib for evaluation, which was an important centre of learning at that time. There was much discussion on the volume for a long time. One line of thought was to let the banis remain in separate volumes for students and for scholars to study them in depth; another was to divide them into two volumes separating the bani of the tenth guru from the history; yet another set of scholars wanted to keep the book as it is excluding the charitars and the eleven stories after the *Zafarnama* only; some others maintained that the granth be divided into various books containing each subject separately.

The discussions carried on endlessly without reaching any decision. In the meantime, Massa Ranghar's highhandedness in the Darbar Sahib disturbed everyone. In 1797, Bhai Mehtab Singh of Bikaner took it upon himself to settle Massa Ranghar once and for all. When he stayed in Dam Dama, the Panth sought his views on the *Dasam Granth*. He replied that if he returned safely after killing Massa Ranghar then the granth should remain as it is, and if he was defeated then it may be separated into various pothis. Bhai Mehtab Singh got a royal reception from the masses when he returned after killing Massa Ranghar. Thus the *Dasam Granth* remained as it was originally designed by Bhai Mani Singh.

Another beed (volume) of *Dasam Granth* was written by Bhai Sukha Singh, granthi of Patna Sahib, in which he included the Chhakey Bhagti Satotar. Many more versions came up from time to time, but the most accepted versions are Bhai Mani Singh's, and Bhai Sukha Singh's volumes.

Thus the *Dasam Granth* remained a subject of controversy from its inception, though the discord is not so much on the contents as it is on the compilation. Many students have done research on the subject and have been awarded degrees of Doctorates of Literature, from various universities, but the authorship of the *Dasam Granth* has not been decided one way or the other, with any amount of certainty. Some of them have proved logically that the entire *Dasam Granth* is the creation of Guru Gobind Singh, while others maintain that only five of the banis in the *Dasam Granth* are composed by him and the others are by other poets. Some of the notable researchers are Shamsher Singh Ashok, Rattan Singh Jaggi and Dharampal Ashta. They have done a lot of research but no one has been able to establish the truth with any certainty.

The outcome of this controversy is that the *Dasam Granth* has faded into insignificance. It is placed for reading along with the *Guru Granth Sahib* only in the historical gurudwaras such as Takht Sri Dam Dama Sahib, Takht Sri Patna Sahib, and Sri Sachkhand Nanded, and a few other takhts. In all the other gurudwaras *Dasam Granth* is nowhere to be seen. The result is that the common people are not even aware of the existence of *Dasam Granth*.

Bachitar Natak, The Resplendent Drama as it has also been called, forms part of the *Dasam Granth*. It is also available in a separate book in Punjabi, and contains the original text along with the translation. It has 14 chapters and 471 verses.

The first few chapters are devoted to the invocation to God. Strangely the khadag, the sword as the personification of that Power, Shakti, is invoked. The Almighty God is praised in different ways recounting His attributes, qualities and talents. It goes on to say that life is not immortal and man must live consciously knowing that all will come to an end one day. The third and fourth chapters trace the lineage of the Bedis and the Sodhis. The fifth chapter describes the life of Guru Nanak, his birth in a Bedi family, and his successors in the tradition of a newly found way of life, Sikhism.

It is in the sixth chapter, which is autobiographical, that the verse, '*Apni katha*', appears. The rest of the chapter describes the other messengers who failed to do His bidding. The seventh chapter has only three verses, describing his conception in Triveni, his birth in Patna, his early upbringing in Punjab, and the martyrdom of his father, Guru Tegh Bahadur when he was barely nine years old.

All the historical events connected with the present life of Guru Gobind Singh begin with Chapter eight. The chapter describes the battle with Fateh Shah of Srinagar Garhwal, at Bhangani near Paunta along with hill chiefs, and the victory over him, which brought about a welcome change in the fortunes of the Sikhs. The ninth chapter explains the reason why the guru had to join forces with the hill rajas in order to resist the onslaughts of the Mughal Emperor, Aurangzeb. The tenth chapter describes how Rustom Khan, son of Dilawar Khan was sent to subdue Guru Gobind Singh but had to taste defeat at the hands of Guru's valiant Sikhs. While retreating Rustom Khan's army destroyed Barwa, a village on the way.

The eleventh chapter consisting of 69 verses, describes the battle with Hussaini. After the defeat of his son Rustom Khan, Lahore's subedar Dilawar Khan sent his Gulam (slave) Hussaini to subdue Guru Gobind Singh. Raja Bhim Chand assisted Hussaini while some hill rajas helped the guru. A fierce battle was fought. Hussaini and many hill rajas were killed. It was a victory for the guru's valiant Sikhs again. The twelfth chapter describes the wrath of Dilawar Khan, Subedar of Lahore. He could not bear to hear of the death of Hussaini and the humiliating defeat of the Mughals. He collected a bigger army under the command of Rustom Khan. Jujhar Singh Hara and Chander Rai were appointed to assist him. When Raj Singh Jasawalia came to know about it, he accepted the challenge, and gave a good fight to Rustom Khan. In this battle Rustom Khan was defeated and his assistants Jujhar Singh and Chander Rai were killed.

The thirteenth chapter describes the time when Aurangzeb

was in the south. He came to know about Dilawar Khan's successive defeats against the Guru, so he sent his son Mauzam (Bahadur Shah 1st) to Punjab. Mauzam led a large army and attacked Punjab. He started killing people indiscriminately. Because of this, people got scared and ran to the safety of the hills. He destroyed village after village. All those who had deserted the Guru also got killed.

In in the last chapter of 11 verses, the Guru praises and thanks the almighty God who saved his followers in difficult situations.

Adbhut gat bhagatan dikhrai
Sabh sankat te laye bachai 11 1 11

Thus in *Bachitar Natak*, the life history of the first 32 years of Guru Gobind Singh is given. The battle scenes are so powerfully depicted that one feels as if one is taking part in the battle. The sounds of striking swords and other arms are well matched with the sound of words and some instances have been shown in word pictures. Sometimes a humorous touch is also given. Two main points on which more emphasis is given are, first, that Guru Gobind Singh did tapasya (penance) at Hemkunt for a long time and Wahe Guru was pleased with him and commanded him to go to the world (kaliyug) with a special mission. The mission was to uphold righteousness and to serve humanity – equally to work for the poor, the oppressed and the downtrodden. God also spoke that whenever He had sent messengers on similar missions, they had failed because they became so powerful that they completely forgot their mission. Instead they wore the mantle of God themselves.

Second point which Guru Gobind Singh has emphasized is that if a common man, who is ordinarily very timid and weakminded, can be infused with courage and self-confidence, he will surely perform deeds of valour in the battlefield His inspired Sikhs, who came mostly from lower castes, first fought with the hill rajas and later on took on even the mighty Mughals, and won glory. There is a saying that one Sikh can fight one and a quarter lakh men in the battlefield. Guru Gobind Singh also claimed that he can get a hawk killed by a sparrow and this has been proved many times.

The main question is, what was the aim of writing this chapter. He explained that he did tough tapasya at Hemkunt and because of it Wahe Guru sent him in this world.

a. Did he desire that the place of tapasya be discovered later on by his followers and a magnificent gurudwara be built where he performed tapaysa in his previous life?
b. Or should his followers also leave all the worldly affairs and do tapasya like him in a secluded place, away from the marketplace? This does not seem plausible since the teaching of Shri *Guru Granth Sahib* emphasises the life of a karamyogi. *Kirat karna*, *wand chhakna*, *naam japna* (work hard, share with others and remember the name of God)are the three tenets that sum up the Sikh way of life.
c. Should earlier birth be considered?

There are many ifs and buts for which there are no answers in any of the religious books.

The fact remains that a magnificent gurudwara has come up

at Hemkunt and a lot of followers of the faith reach there, facing many hardships and difficulties, to seek His blessings. It is also true that the deity worshipped in the Hemkunt Gurudwara is the *Guru Granth Sahib*, as everywhere else, but the hills lend a different charm to the place.

Jithe jai bahe mera satguru so than suhawa Ram Raje
Gur sikhi so than bhaliya lai thood mukh lawa 11 (War Asa 18)

Wherever my Guru is present that place becomes holy.
Gursikhi has found the place and bows low to take its dust.

DUSHT DAMAN

Destroyer of Unholy Spirits and Demons is the name that has been connected with Guru Gobind Singh. Whenever the name Dusht Daman is used it pertains to the tenth Guru, that is Guru Gobind Singh. Some devout authors have titled their booklets on Hemkunt 'Dusht Daman'. But if we continue with our research, we find that this name was first mentioned by Bhai Santokh Singh Churamani in his voluminous Sikh history titled *Sri Gur Pratap Suraj Granth* commonly known as *Suraj Prakash Granth*. Bhai Santokh Singh started writing this granth in 1835 A.D. and completed it in 1843 but it carries the date line of 1835 A.D.

Bhai Santokh Singh was a great scholar of that time. He spent

DASAM GRANTH

COMPARATIVE CHART OF VARIOUS VERSIONS

Bhai Mani Singh Wali Bir	Hoti Bagh Gurudwara Wali Bir	Sangrur Wali Bir	Patna Sahib Wali Bir	Granth published by Bhai Jwahar Singh Kripal Singh
Jaap	Jaap	Jaap	Jaap	Jaap
Bachitar Natak	Bachitar Natak	Shastarnam Mala	Alal Ustat	Alal Ustat
Chandi Charitar - 1	Chandi Charitar - 1	Akal Ustai	Sway - 32	Bachitar Natak
Chandi Charitar - 2	Chandi Charitar - 2	Bachitar Natak	Bachitar Natak	Chandi Charitar - 1
Chubis Avtar	Chubis Avtar	Chandi Charitar - 1	Chubis Avtar	Chandi Charitar - 2
Brahamavtar	Brahamavtar	Chubis Avtar	Chandi Charitar - 1	Var Shri Bhagoti Ki
Rudravtar	Rudravtar	Brahamavtar	Brahamavtar	Gian Parbudh
Paras Nath	Paras Nath	Rudravtar	Gian Parbudh	Chubis Avtar
Shasternam Mala	Shasternam Mala	Gian Parbudh	Chandi Charitar - 2	Brahamavtar
Gian Parbudh	Akal Ustai	Charitru Pakhiyan	Rudravtar	Rudravtar
Akal Ustai	Gian Parbudh	Sanshar Sukhnand	Bishan Pade	Ramkali Patshaih 10
Var Purgaki	Var Durga Ki	Var Nalkos Ki	Chakka Bhagotika	Saway
Charitru Pakhiyan	Charitru Pakhiyan	Chaka Bhagoti Ji Ka	Shastar Nan Mala	Khalsh Naam Saway
Zafarnama	Asphutak Kabit	Bishan Pade	Var Durga Ki	Shastar Nan Nala
Hidyatan Sahit	Saway - 33	Zafarnama (Both in Gurmukhi & Persian)	Charitro Pakhiyan	Charitro Pakhiyan
Sad	Bishan Pade (Shabad Hazare)	Sway - 33	Asphutak Kabit	Zafarnama
	Sad	Asphutak Kabit	Bhagwat Gita	Hikyat
	Zafarnama (Gurmukhi & Persian)	Sirlekh to Bina	Sanshar Sukhpana	Shabad (In Rags)
		Kuoh Pad	Var Naokoo Ki	
			Var Bhagoti Ki	
			Zafarnama (Gurmukhi)	

his earlier days at Buriya (Ambala) and later on with S. Sant Singh of Amritsar and learnt a lot from him as the latter was an authority on Sikhism. After some time, he moved to Patiala and started writing. He won the favour of Maharaja Karam Singh. Later on, the mother of Maharaja Udey Singh of Kaithal, a small state adjoining Patiala, now in Dist Kurukshetra of Haryana, asked him to become his tutor. He started teaching Maharaja Udey Singh who was just an infant.

It was at that time, when he was enjoying royal patronage, that he considered writing the life history of the ten gurus and started collecting material from various sources. The outcome was *Suraj Prakash Granth* written in Braj Bhasha, the language prevalent at that time in literature. Soon afterwards Braj Bhasha disappeared from Punjab, and is no longer understood by the Punjabis. Many years later, Bhai Vir Singh took it upon himself to bring the book to the masses. So he started translating it into Punjabi. He published it with footnotes and meanings of difficult words. This granth consists of more than 6000 pages.

The word Dusht Daman has been used many times between pages 4176 to 4183 in Bhai Vir Singh's compilation. There is no reference from where Bhai Santokh Singh got this word. There is no mention of any other book or granth from where it may have been taken. Dusht Daman is given in *Gur Pratap Suraj Granth* in Ras 11, Anshu 22. The heading of sub-chapter (anshu) 51 is Brahma Narrating the Old Stories (Brahma da Puratan Katha Sunana).

Jada chahio chit, tada tyagon lakhon samat jara na aaye
Tapan taphon aati ugar tej hoi dusht daman nij nam dharaye

Sangat bane asankh anik thal, mam saroop hi he jis bhaye
Ithi bes main bane raho nit 1 Jab kab janh kanh karav sahai
11 8 11 (p. 4176)

What ever you feel like doing please do it.
You will not become old for centuries to come.
You pray, you will become a great man.
Keep your name as Dusht Daman.
You will get a lot of following where ever you go
but they will represent me.
You stay in this condition forever,
and if you want any assistance,
I will come and help you.

Dusht adharmi son kar sanghar marg dharm rahe chhit chhaye
Jit kit haten malechhan gan ko badhe yudh priya judh machaye
Dusht Daman te devi sun kar kahi bhavikhat baat sunaye
Purab bhag chuterathe jug ko tabe samo aiso bun aaye
11 9 11 (p. 4177)

All the devils, the non-believers, should be destroyed.
Everyone should praise God and keep on fighting the devil.
After listening to Dusht Daman, the Devi predicts
That this period will come in the first part of the kalyug
When all the devils will be destroyed.

Bhai so lope bhagwati tehn te 1
Dusht Daman nij naam dharaye
Tapsi purakh gayo pit ke dhig, darshan dekhit sis nawae
Puter bilokat harkhit hoye kar durga bar lakh baak alaye
Shakti kar parsan ho sat taw, bur linis kar ke chit chaye 11 11 11

Bhagwati named him Dusht Daman
And he paid his respects to her.
Durga became very happy and blessed him
Saying all your wishes will be fulfilled.

Dhun gambhir saghan mridula bahu bole baak mund muskan
Dusht Daman, sun parathme upjiyo, karyo tapisar ne mum dhiyan
Apno tap parbhavit kinas kaaran karibo judh mahan
Yante anash ahen taon hamri tapey mahan tapkaway na saman//15//

With a smile on her face and in a serious tone
She told Dusht Daman to fight big battles to kill the devils.
Now that you are my part, do such tapasya,
Which no other living being has done in this world.

Sun ke Dusht Daman kar jore, tahan jaan mein bighan bisal
Anik bhant ki hohen prabirta ar boh badhyo kali ko kaal
Charan aap ke surat chubhi mum, tikyo aadhik man prem rasal
Chit menh nahin jaan abhilakha iik ras rachto saroop sambhal
(//17//, p. 4184)

After hearing, Dusht Daman, with folded hands said
'It is next to impossible to reach there.
There are many difficulties on the way
And people are under the influence of Kalyug.
I am fully devoted to you and will always pray to you.
And think about you.
I have got no desire to leave you.'

Iim keh Dusht Daman koh boh bidh apne ank bikhe bethae
Main apna sut tohe niwajeo panth prachur karieh jug jae
Sri Nanak ki jot mahan bal nawam sreer bikhe parvishae
So tapsi hai pita toharo shantmati sabh so sumtae 11 20 11

After saying all that, she made Dusht Daman sit next to her.
I have made you my son.
Now please go in the world and preach a new religion (panth).
The ninth Guru, your father has taken the form of Guru Nanak.
He is a great saint and believes in peaceful life.

Iim keh mastak sunghat dekhat jim pit te sut kite sidhai
Mirdual madhur sarath pursharath sharey bhare shubh baak sunae
Sun ke Dusht Daman hoe thadon haath jor kar bine alaye
Panth chalah tub jagat majharo jub howo tum aap sahai 11 23 11

After saying this, she kissed his forehead and bid him farewell.
She blessed him in many ways

After listening to all that, Dusht Daman stood up
Folded his hands and prayed
Only with your help, the new religion (panth) will come up and progress.

The above passages have been quoted from Bhai Santokh Singh's *Gur Pratap Suraj Granth*, and it is obvious that he has used the expression Dusht Daman many times and has written about the previous birth of Guru Gobind Singh.

On the other hand there is a book called *Markande Puran* in which Dusht Daman is the name given to Rishi Modhasha. He helped Durga by destroying devils and in the olden times he was called Dusht Daman. As a matter of fact, Dusht Daman is a name given by Bhai Santokh Singh only, as there is no other reference anywhere.

the quest

Jithe jaya bahe mera satguru
so thaan sohawa ram raje

MARG GOBIND

Whenever we visualize the search for Hemkunt by earlier travellers and pilgrims, our imagination goes back to the days of the great difficulties they must have encountered in the Himalayas. What great difficulties Pandit Tara Har Narotam must have faced when he went across the Himalayas looking for the spot called Hemkunt, as at that time nobody had heard about the place and one wonders how he hit upon the exact place as there were no locations or references anywhere except in *Bachitar Natak*. But Pandit Tara Har Narotam mentioned it briefly in his book *Gur Tirath Sangrah* on page 91. The photo block of the same print is reproduced overleaf.

He mentions, "Six *koh* below Gandh Madan Parbat (Badrinath) is Pandukeshwar and its pujari takes pilgrims to

Lohpal (Hemkunt). It was a known fact that the local people referred to the spot as Lohpal or Lokpal, or even Lokpaleshwar.

Sardar Partap Singh went there in 1934 and mentions it in his book *Meri Parbat Pherian*. But it was Sant Sohan Singh of Tehri (Garhwal) who reached there earlier. The difference between the two was that Sant Sohan Singh went alone and was searching in the dark, so to speak, whereas Partap Singh went with his friends and knew where to go. Before he started he had collected all the details about Hemkunt from Sant Sohan Singh in Amritsar.

There is little doubt that these roads, mule paths, tracks must have existed since ages as there must have been some pedlars in olden days as well. The question was how to overcome the difficulties on the way. One had to be away from home for months to go to the holy Badrinath. No conveyance was available and the distance had to be covered on foot all the way from the foothills. Pandit Tara Har Narotam has written in his book that

This sketch is taken from *Gur Tirath Sangrah*. From the sketch it is clear that Pandit Tara Har Narotam had visited this place in 1884 as all the details have been given on how to reach the place.

a road existed at Pandukeshwar. More likely, it must have been a mule track only.

From the olden Hindu Granths, it is known that in Uttarakhand, a famous Dham called Badrinath existed. There are no records available about how and when this temple came into existence. Since it is mentioned in the Vedas, one can hazard a guess. And that explains the existence of the path.

Badrinath is famous because of the Vishnu temple. Since it is adjoining Tibet, where Budhism was the prevalent religion, there must have been some influence in this area. The story goes that Buddhists had uprooted the deity and had thrown it in Narad Kund where it had been lying for years.

In the eighth century, Buddhism came under direct attack by the Brahmins. Budhist and Jain temples were demolished and the Jains and Buddhists had to flee and take shelter in the neighbouring countries. One gets details of it in *Shankar Digvijay Granth* and *Vividharth* by Dr Bhagwan Das.

Shankaracharya hailed from Kerala, a state in South India, and was a Namboodri Brahmin, who considered themselves as pure Aryans. Shankaracharya visited Badrinath and on the way he demolished all the Buddhist temples with the help of Raja Sadhnawa's army. He started praying at Badrinath temple. One day he dreamt that a statue of the presiding deity was lying in Narad Kund. And that he would be granted his wish if he were to retrieve the statue and instal it in the sanctum sanctorum. He retrieved it and again installed it in the temple making it a Hindu temple.

All these events took place in the eighth century and people from all over India started the pilgrimage to this holy place. If we believe in these events, then it is sure that the road or path also existed to Badrinath from the eighth century if not much earlier. It is also known that people used to go to Kailash Mansarovar through this route from times immemorial.

Records show that Hemkunt was popularly known as Lokpal. Though this place was not as famous as Badrinath, still people used to visit this place at least thrice a year. They went there for puja with a pure heart and this tradition is still going on. So it is a fact that people used to traverse on these roads, though it was very difficult especially for the people who were not accustomed to the hilly terrain. But as time passed, lines of transport and communication improved and people found it easier to move about, and started visiting in large numbers.

People made narrow paths by the bank of the river, which were later converted to mule tracks. In the olden days there were no means to blast the mountains or make the tunnels, so the easiest way was to move along the rivers. Roads were built when the government felt the need to do so. After the Indo-China war in 1962, there was need for better means of transport and communication for defense purposes, so more and better roads were built.

There was a time when it used to take months to make a pilgrimage from Hardwar to Badrinath but now one can make this trip in a day or two by car, or even by bus.

But the last 18 km to Hemkunt, one still has to traverse on foot in very difficult terrain. Those who have undertaken this yatra, can never forget the climb from Gobind Ghat to Hemkunt and back. It is just strong will and determination that keep one moving. At least for these four days, one forgets all about the worldly affairs and remembers God from the core of the heart and the Almighty seems to be near and watching. It is conceivable that a road can be built from Gobind Ghat to Hemkunt also. But is it worth it? It will not only cause environmental damage but turn this holy place into a mere picnic spot. It is a matter of argument whether the road should be built from Gobind Ghat or one should encounter some difficulties to reach that place.

Pandit Tara Har Narotam in his book *Gur Tirath Sangrah* has written: "If some Guru's beloved, Raja Babu Sikh, after spending five/seven thousand rupees could build a road from the edge of Pandkeshwar bridge to the temple near Mahakali which is tapasya place of Guruji (Guru Gobind Singh), then it is sure that people will prefer to come here (Hemkunt) as the distance will be only 8 kos. The person who will build this road will become famous and will do a very good job by bringing pilgrims to this sacred place."

Had Narotam ji been alive today, he would have been surprised to see that what he had visualized more than a century ago has almost come true now. Let us see what the future holds for us and what progress will be made in this century to bring millions of devotees to this holy land.

LOHPAL – LOKPAL – LOKPALESHWAR

Hemkunt has been known by many different names down the centuries. Among them the familiar ones are: Lohpal, Lokpal and Lokpaleshwar. Bhai Kahan Singh of Nabha has explained the meaning of Lohpal-Lokpal and Lokpaleshwar in his *Mahan*

Kosh (*Encyclopaedia of the Sikh Literature*) p. 1072-73.

Lohpal- Keeper of prison, see Lokpal
Lokpal- Almighty God who looks after all the things
Lokpaleshwar- Head of the Lokpal means Kartar (Almighty)

Pandit Tara Har Narotam writes in his book *Gur Tirath Sangrah* about the search Hemkunt on pages 91-92

> *Pul de sameep hi Alaknanda mein Bhoti Ganga milti hai. Pul pe lakh Bhoti ke saje hath jate hi tin kos pe ek gaon hai. Wahan aur pul hai us pai Lakh Bhoti Ganga ke khabe haath jate teen kos pe Bhoti Ganga sath Lohpal ke jal ka sangam hai, enhan se chadhai lagti hai.So do kos ka rasta kathan hai.Pandkeshar ka pujari Lohpal mein le jata hai. Lohpal mein jal ka talau hai. So sawa sau kadam chaura hai.Aadh kos pake ka lamba hai-asal main nam Lokpaleshwar hai. Kahe te woh sarowar lokpalon Ka hai. Lokpalon ke sarower kinare wasi mahandev ka naam Lokpaleshwar hai. Badri mahatam mein iis tirath ke sameep jaa kar mul mooter datum kurla thukne ka bada sankoch likha hai. Talab ke jal mein koi daka gere rikhijaan panchhion ka roop dhar uda le jate hain. Maud gram, Pandkeshwar, Joshimath, Ghumhar Chati, neti aadi gramon ke parbati lok wahan ki puja karte hain. Isi than se baith ke guru ji ne purab janam mein kalkali mein chit lagaye tap kiya.*

> Bhoti Ganga meets Alakhnanda near the bridge. On the right bank of Bhoti, there is a village about 3 kos (kos is a bit longer than a mile) from the bridge. There is another bridge there, on the left side of Bhoti Ganga, at about three kos. Lohpal river and Bhoti Ganga meet at this point and then starts the climb. Two kos climb is very difficult. Pandukeshwar priest escorts you to Lohpal. There is a lake at Lohpal. It is 100-125 feet wide. It is good half a kos in length. The actual name is Lokpaleshwar. Why it is so because the lake is of Lokpalon ka (who takes care of everyone). Mahadev who lives on the bank of Lokpal is called Lokpaleshwar. In the Badri mountain the bank of Lokpal is called Lokpaleshwar. Badri mahatma has forbidden people to urinate, wash mouth or even spit there. If any foreign object falls in the lake, saints in the guise of mysterious birds remove it at once. Villagers of Mana village, Pandukeshwar, Joshimath, Ghumhar Chatti and Neti come to this place to worship. At this place, in olden days, Guru Gobind Singh had mediated and done tap.

From the above it is clear that the place where the guru meditated and did tap is called Lohpal, Lokpal or Lokpleshwar. But now it is known all over the world as Hemkunt. Yet, surprisingly, neither Guru Gobind Singh in his *Bachitar Natak* nor Pandavas in *Mahabharat* have named this place as Lokpal, Lohpal or Lokpaleshwar.

ਤੀਰਥਃ

ਕੇਬਚਨੋਂਸੇਮੇਲਕੇਲਿਖਤੇਹੈਂ।ਭਾਰਤਮੇਂਹੇਮਕੂੰਟਪਰਬਤ ੯੧
ਸ੍ਰਿੰਗਕੇਸਮੀਪਲਿਖਾਹੈ।ਯਤੋ ਹੇਮਕੂਟਸੁਮੇਰਕਾਕਮ
ਨਹੀਂ।ਗੁਰੂਜੀਨੇਲਿਖਾਹੈ ਹੇਮਕੂਟਪਰਬਤਜਹਾਂਹੈਤ
ਹਾਂਤਿਸਕੇਸਮੀਪਸਪਤਸ੍ਰਿੰਗਸੋਭਾਪਾਵਤਾਹੈ।ਜਿਸਮੇ
ਰਾਜਪਾਂਡੂਨੇਜੋਗਕਮਾਯਾਹੈ।ਉਸੀਕੇਸਮੀਪਹਮਨੇਤ
ਪਕੀਆਕਹਾਹੈ।ਤੁਮੇਤਮੇਤਪਕਰਨਾਜੀਲਿਖਾ
ਇਸਕੀਸਪਸਟਕਥਾਐਸੇਹੈ।ਜਿਸਕੇਊਪਰਬਦਰੀ
ਨਾਰਾਇਣਕਾਮੰਦਰਹੈ।ਉਸਪਰਬਤਕਾਨਾਮਗੰਧਮਾਦਨ
ਹੈ।ਗੰਧਮਾਦਨਸੇਛੀਕੋਸਨੀਚੇਕੇਪਰਬਤਕਾਨਾਮਸਤ
ਸ੍ਰਿੰਗਹੈ।ਉਸਮੇਪਾਂਡੂਨੇਜੋਗਕੀਆ।ਅਬਵਹਾਂਪੰਡੁਕੇ
ਸਰਨਾਮਬਸਤਾਹੈ।ਬਦਰੀਨਾਰਾਇਣਕੀਯਾਤ੍ਰਾਸਭ
ਉਹਾਂਕੋਹੋਕਰਜਾਤੀਹੈ।ਕਿਨਾਰੇਜਾਨੇਕੋਮਸਤਾਨਗੀਸ
ਤਸ੍ਰਿੰਗਸੇਆਠਕੋਸਊਪਰਗੁਰੂਜੀਨੇਤਪਕੀਆ।ਸੋ
ਅਤੀਸਪਾਦਕਰਤੇਹੈਂ।ਪੰਡੁਕੇਸਰਸੇਏਕਮੀਲਨੀਚੇਸ
ਰਕਸਮੀਪਅਲਕਨੰਦਾਗੰਗਾਕਾਪੁਲਹੈ।ਪੁਲਕੇਸ
ਮੀਪਗੀਅਲਕਨੰਦਾਮੇਛੋਟੀਗੰਗਾਮਿਲਤੀਹੈ ਪੁਲ
ਪੈਲਖਛੋਟੀਕੇਸੰਗੇਹਾਥਜਾਤੇਤੀਨਕੋਸਪੈਏਕਗਾਉਂ
।ਦਾ।ਐਸਪੁਲਹੈ ਉਸਪੈਲਖਛੋਟੀਗੰਗਾਕੇਸੰਗੇਹਾ
ਥਜਾਤੇਤੀਨਕੋਸਪੈਛੋਟੀਗੰਗਾਸਾਥ ਲੋਹਪਾਲਕੇਜਲ
ਕਾਸੰਗਮਹੈ।ਈਹਾਂਸੇਚੜ੍ਹਾਈਲਗਤੀਹੈ।ਸੋਦੋਕੋਸਠਾ
ਤਾਕਠਨਹੈ।ਪੰਡੁਕੇਸਰਕਾਪੁਜਾਰੀਲੋਹਪਾਲਐਲੋਸਾ
ਤਾਏਮਲੋਹਪਾਲਮੇਸਲਕਾਤਲਾਵਹੈ।ਸੋਸਤ੍ਹਾਏਕ

This page is taken from Gur Tirath Sangrah.

But one of the historians has written about this place as "this holy place Lohpal has been in existence since Satyug. This is mentioned in *Sakand Puran* (ch 8 salok 20) which proclaims, "Among all the sacred places, the Almighty God has himself laid the foundation stone of Lokpal."

Mention of Lokpal in *Sakand Puran* might be correct. But it is doubtful whether the religious story (Sakhi), where almighty God transforms Himself into Mahakal and comes to this place and kills the demon called Bali, is believed to be anywhere near the truth.

In *Guru Nanak Dev Ji de safran de atlas* (Atlas about Guru Nanak Dev Ji's travels), Guru Nanak is said to have visited this place in his first udasi, his first voyage. And while going to Joshimath, he went to Kedarnath and Badrinath also. It is also mentioned that he has been to Lokpal where he met rishis and munis and had discussions with them. Later on he met Kaksamundh, and this mountain is very close to Lokpal, Hemkunt.

Pandit Tara Har Narotam *Gur Tirath Sangrah* has further written pp. 95-96:

> Krishna and Arjun came to this place to get fire brand weapons. This is mentioned in Mahabharat in 80th chapter. Lots of soldiers surrounded Abhimanu, son of Arjun, and trapped him in Chakarbihu, and King Jaidarath of Sindu Desh chopped his head off with a sword. On hearing about his son's death Arjun vowed to kill King Jaidarath by the next day, or he would kill himself.

> Yudishtar told Krishna about Arjun's vow. 'If Arjun dies then our victory will be worse than defeat, so please find a way to save Arjun,' he pleaded. Thus Krishna called Arjun and told him to meditate in seclusion on Mahakal, and Jaidarath will be killed. They then prepared to go to bring the bow and arrow with which Mahakal had killed the Devils (Asur). Krishna caught hold of Arjun's hand and flew away. Mahakal was very happy and said that they could take the bow and arrow from the bottom of the lake. When Arjun and Krishna went to collect the weapons from the lake, they were transformed into snakes with thousand heads, which rose from the lake. On hearing the praise of Mahadev, the weapons came near the shore in their original form. Arjun and Krishan picked them up and took them to Mahakal. They learnt from Mahakal how to use these weapons. Next day Arjun killed Jaidarath with the same weapon." It is further written that Lokpal tirath is near Salinder, on the tip of Maha Mandir Parbat.

In a nutshell, Narotam has written that Krishna and Arjun had come all the way from Kurukshetra to Lokpal during the great war of Mahabharat. Mahakal used to stay at this place. They took the weapon *(Dhanush ban)* from him, learnt how to use it, returned, and killed Jaidrath the next day and took revenge.

It is said that Lokpal is also mentioned in *Waman Puran, Narad Puran* and *Brahamand Puran* besides *Sakand Puran.*

In addition to Shatsring where Pandu king had done penance, and Sapat Sring in *Bachitar Natak*, there seems to be another mountain called Tung Shatsring as described by Narotam in his book.

the pathfinders

Gursikhi so thaan bhalya, lai dhoor mukhlawa

SANT SOHAN SINGH

Pandit Tara Har Narotam was the pioneer who first set foot on the place which is now known as Hemkunt. He described the place in detail in his book *Gur Tirath Sangrah* in 1884, but his findings didn't gain currency. Sant Sohan Singh of Tehri Garhwal, came into prominence because he was able to construct a Gurudwara there. He had to face many difficulties, but he had the backing of Bhai Vir Singh, so he succeeded in his mission.

It is surprising that though Bhai Vir Singh published *Kalgidhar Chamatkar* in 1925, nobody got the inspiration to search and identify the place where Guru Gobind Singh did tapasya in his previous birth. It is equally astonishing that though Bhai Vir Singh wrote about Hemkunt he never made an attempt to find it himself. He never visited the area nor did he send any individual or team to locate the place. It is not understood why he did not take up this mission himself. But when Sant Sohan Singh read *Kalgidhar Chamatkar*, and was inspired to locate the site that was Guru Gobind Singh's tapasthan in his previous birth, he approached Bhai Vir Singh and received all the encouragement and money from him.

Anyhow it was Sant Sohan Singh who went in search of it and it is his name that will be associated with the search for Hemkunt Sahib. The first time he went in 1933 he failed. But he persevered and again went in 1934. This time he was able to locate it. He came back and informed Bhai Vir Singh and insisted that a gurudwara should be built at the Tapasthan to which Bhai Vir Singh agreed. He also gave him Rs 2100 along with a copy of *Guru Granth Sahib* and all the essential things required there initially. He kept on writing in *Khalsa Samachar* about the discovery and appealed to the Sangat for financial help. In 1937, a gurudwara measuring 10'x10' size along with a 3 ft verandah was constructed and Nishan Sahib was installed there.

Sant Sohan Singh was a local granthi in a gurudwara in Tehri (Garhwal), a hilly place, located in Uttaranchal. It is said that he was a religious teacher in the army before he was appointed granthi in the Tehri gurudwara. In spite of all the efforts, his earlier life history could not be traced and nothing more is known about him. As per Bhai Nanda Singh, who assisted him, he was a tall man and had lost sight in one eye. He was a very religious man with strong will power. It is a pity that nobody has kept any records about him or written anything about him.

It is not very clear whether Sant Sohan Singh had ever heard

The first gurudwara 10" x10" with 3 feet verandah, which was constructed in 1936. Major General Harkirat Singh, under whose supervision the design of the present Gurudwara was approved, is on the extreme left.

about Pandit Tara Har Narotam or his book *Gur Tirath Sangrah*, as a complete sketch of the place and guidelines of how to reach there have been explained in detail therein. He started on foot from Rishikesh, as there were no metalled roads beyond it. From here one had to undertake the journey on foot on paths and mule tracks made by yatris of Badrinath, Kedarnath or even of Kailash Mansarovar. There were small huts called chattis on the way, at a convenient distance for shelter where rations etc. were available and arrangements to cook food. Lots of yatris used to undertake the pilgrimage to Badrinath, approximately 300 km from Rishikesh. There were no records available, and no one to forewarn the yatris about all the difficulties and problems they could encounter. The only guide happened to be S. Partap Singh's book, *Merian Parbat Pherian*, published by National Book Shop when he went there in 1934. Sant Sohan Singh just lived on roasted gram and gur (jaggery), the only things he had carried with him. He visited many places including Badrinath, made enquiries about Hemkunt everywhere, but as no one had heard this name before, no one was able to guide him. He failed in his mission and came back disappointed.

But he did not lose heart, and kept his morale high. And he decided to go in search for it again, the next summer. There is a possibility that he might have talked to various people and maybe even requested them to accompany him but obviously no one agreed to take the risk. As per the records available, he embarked on the marathon mission all by himself. In a pamphlet published by Hemkunt Trust, Kanpur in 2002, which does not bear the author's or printer's name and is titled "Hemkunt Parbat hai Jahan, Sapat Sring Sobhit Hai Tahan", the unknown author claims on page 6, that he was accompanied by Shri Baba Kartar Singh Bedi. But neither Nanda Singh nor anybody else has verified it. The source of this information is also not mentioned. Had he been with Santji, both of them would have met Bhai Vir Singh and he would have mentioned it thereafter in his writings. It is more likely that Baba Bedi also visited the place sometimes later.

In the summer of 1934, Sant Sohan Singh prepared himself, for the second expedition. He collected items of daily needs and rations and started for Badrinath. In Badrinath, he enquired from many people about Hemkunt. But there was no one to guide him. So he decided to go back to Joshimath, with the aim of

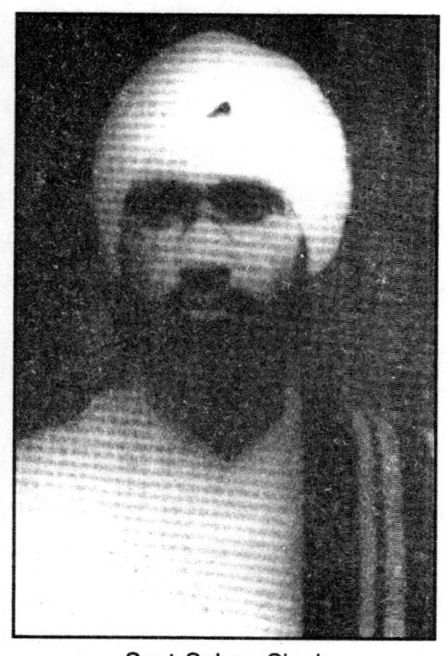

Sant Sohan Singh

making enquires. But due to some unknown reason he had to spend the night at Pandukeshwar. Early in the morning when he was ready to move to Joshimath, he saw a group of local men and women, well attired and ready to move to some place. He was surprised and asked them where they were going. They told him that at a distance of 14 miles, there is a holy place called Lokpal and they were going there for a holy dip on this auspicious day. They further told him that the journey was very tough and arduous, and that they could not reach that place in one day, so they had to spend a night in a village on the way. Curious to find out more about this place, Sant Sohan Singh decided to accompany them. At that time there was a ropeway bridge on the river Alakhnanda. It was very embarassing for Sant Sohan Singh as he had to cross the river with the help of villagers whereas others crossed it without any help. From here they all moved in a group at a slow pace and by evening reached a village called Bhiondar. At that time Rattan Singh Chauhan was the headman (lumbardar) of the village. After introducing himself, Sant Sohan Singh spent the night at his house. In the morning Rattan Singh and his son

Nanda Singh also decided to go with the party and all of them started the tough climb. At a place called Ghagria (now Gobind Dham), about three miles from this village, Sant Sohan Singh was surprised to see that the villagers discarded their colourful clothes and changed to very simple ones. They even removed their footwear and started walking bare foot. Sant Sohan Singh was very much impressed with the simplicity, devotion and faith of the villagers.

Sant Sohan Singh found that the going was very tough. There was a very narrow path and at times, even that disappeared. One had to hold on to the bushes to climb up. With great difficulty and with the help of Rattan Singh he finally reached Lokpal. His first impression was of awe and wonder. He had never seen a more beautiful place in all his life. He stood there transfixed. He looked all around at the surroundings. He found a beautiful lake and then he counted the peaks surrounding the lake, and found them to be exactly seven, as mentioned in *Bachitar Natak*. He remained still for a while and imagined that this could be the actual place where Guru Gobind Singh had done tapasya in his previous birth. He tried to get information from the villagers, but they were of no help. After taking a dip in the lake and performing the puja, they left. They insisted that he should accompany them back, as nobody spent the night at that altitude, and that too all alone. But he decided to stay on. He started doing simran. And an idea came to his mind. He got up, folded his hands and sincerely started saying ardas in which he said, 'Oh Almighty God, Oh, Dashmesh Guru, with your blessings and guidance I have been led to this place. Now please give me some concrete evidence whether this is the same place, where you performed the tapsaya in your previous birth and if so, which was the exact spot where you sat and did the tapasya.' He completed the ardas and bent down in earnest to touch the ground with his forehead. When he opened his eyes, he found an old man approaching him. He had a long flowing white beard and was wrapped in a tiger's skin. After seeing Sant Sohan Singh at the spot, he asked, "Khalsa ji, what are you looking for?"

With folded hands, Sant ji paid respect to the Maharishi and said, "Hey Yogeshwar Maharaj, I am searching for the place where Guru Gobind Singh did tapasya in his previous birth."

The Maharishi, pointed to a stone slab and said, "Yes, this is the slab on which Dusht Daman sat and did his tapaysa."

Sant Sohan Singh was overwhelmed with joy. He ran up to the stone slab, touched it with his head to pay respect, embraced it and, overcame with happiness, tears rolled down his cheeks. After some time, he composed himself and thought of asking the Maharishi some more questions. He opened his eyes, got up and looked around for the Maharishi but found that he had already left. He looked for him all around but could not find him. He had just disappeared. Sant Sohan Singh was convinced that this was the real place where Guru Gobind Singh had done the tapaysa as a messenger of the Almighty God had come to certify it. On fulfilling the mission, he had disappeared. He thanked the Almighty God for the same and after saying the ardas again and paying homage, started his climb down and days later reached his home at Tehri, excited and jubilant.

The above version is given as stated by Sant Sohan Singh to Bhai Vir Singh and there are no witnesses to certify it. He used to narrate this story wherever he went in Punjab.

Sant Sohan Singh was fully convinced that the place he had visited was the correct place where Guru Gobind Singh had meditated in his previous birth. He decided that a gurudwara should be built on the spot where Dusht Daman had done tapaysa so his followers could come and pay homage to him. He decided that the place should have Nishan Sahib and all the surrounding hills should echo with the jaikara of the Khalsa 'Jo Bole So Nihal – Sat Sri Akal.' He made big plans. But he soon realized that for all that a lot of money and effort was required, and he was just a poor man with not enough resources for the purpose. He decided to go to every village and town and spread the message of Guru Gobind Singh hoping to collect the money to construct the gurudwara. As the belief goes, if you have faith in Wahe Guru and decide to do some pious work, Wahe Guru helps you to complete the work. He started from Mussoorie, and went to Dehradun, Saharanpur, Ambala, Delhi and right upto Lahore. He told and retold his experience at Hemkunt. But he was not keen to collect small amounts of money. He wanted a single individual or an organization to come forward and take up the task of constructing the gurudwara. One of the devotees told him to contact Bhai Vir Singh in Amritsar and tell him about the discovery as he was the right person who could fulfill his desire.

In late 1934, he reached Wazir Hind Press, in Hall Bazar, Amritsar, where Bhai Vir Singh used to supervise the composing and editing work of *Gur Pratap Suraj Granth.* Bhai Vir Singh received him warmly and listened to him with an open mind. Sant Sohan Singh gave a detailed account of his visit to the mountains in 1933 and then again in 1934. He said that he had discovered the place where Guru Gobind Singh had done his tapaysa in his previous life. He strongly wished to see a gurudwara built on that sacred place. He told him that he was a Nirmala Sadhu and had no money, and in spite of his best efforts he could not find any person or organization to volunteer to take up the project. He further said that, on his part, he would always be readily available for advice and assistance in the construction of the gurudwara.

Bhai Vir Singh congratulated him for discovering the place and assured him that he would help him in every possible way.

There is no doubt that Bhai Vir Singh, who had written about this place in *Shri Kalgidhar Chamatkar*, must have been perplexed. He was a poet and his work was based on imagination. He couldn't imagine that somebody had taken him seriously and had gone to the hills to find the place. He was touched by Sant Sohan Singh's faith and determination. Yet he would have liked to be doubly sure about the authenticity of the place before he went along with Sant Sohan Singh's discovery.

Luckily when they had concluded the discussion, Partap Singh appeared on the scene. He had come to meet Bhai Vir Singh. A schoolteacher by profession, Partap Singh loved the mountains. Bhai Vir Singh knew that he had been to the hills many times. Bhai Vir Singh introduced Partap Singh to Sant Sohan Singh and told him about his discovery of Hemkunt Sahib. Partap Singh asked Sant ji about the place and the latter spoke in detail about all that he had found out. He told him that it was near Badrinath, and with the help of sketches explained how to reach the place. After listening to Sant ji and studying his sketches he became silent. When Bhai Vir Singh asked him about it, Partap

Singh replied, "You are a great statesman and leader of the Sikhs and everybody respects you. Before you decide about this, you must be fully convinced that this is the correct place."

Bhai Vir Singh knew that Partap Singh was fond of trekking in the Himalayas and was an educated man. It must have seemed fortuitous that he arrived just at that moment. There could be no better man than Partap Singh to go there and confirm whatever Sant ji had discovered.

As for Partap Singh, he was only too happy to take on the project.

SARDAR PARTAP SINGH

When I heard of Sardar Partap Singh I made an appointment with him on telephone and reached his house in Vasant Vihar, New Delhi, in March 1999. In his younger days he was a teacher in Amritsar and during summer vacations he used to go to the mountains along with his friends. Later on he joined Central Government service and retired as under-secretary of Government of India. When I met him he was about 90 years old and active physically. He had a remarkable memory. He told me that he had visited Hemkunt in 1934 after Bhai Vir Singh had requested him to do so and that he had written a book named *Merian Parbat Pherian* in Punjabi, which was published by National Book Shop, Chandni Chowk, Delhi. I tried to locate the book, but it was not available in the market or with publishers. So I again met him and he lent me his personal copy and gave me permission to get photostat copies made of pages 123 to 155 of

Gurudwara Shri Hemkunt Management Trust at Rishikesh

Gurudwara Shri Hemkunt Management Trust, Srinagar (Garhwal)

Gurudwara Gobind Ghat

Gurudwara Gobind Dham

On the way. Near Gobind Dham

Approaching Hemkunt Sahib with Brahm kamal in bloom

Hemkunt Sahib with the pentagonal roof

In winter while under construction

Another view in winter

Yatris at the bathing ghat

Surrounded by the seven peaks

A dip in the holy sarovar

the chapter 'Hemkunt Badrinath'. He had only one copy left with him. He had written about his visit to Badrinath and Hemkunt in detail, the difficulties he came across and the report submitted to Bhai Vir Singh.

When Bhai Vir Singh gave him the responsibility of confirming the search made by Sant Sohan Singh, he first read *Bachitar Natak* and then *Gur Tirath Sangrah*. He was convinced that Pandit Tara Har Narotam had visited the place, as he had given his experience in detail, complete with a sketch map (reproduced at p. 80).

Partap Singh contacted his friends and told them about the difficult mission. They made all the preparations, and started in August 1935. After visiting Hardwar, Rishikesh, Dev Prayag, they trekked slowly towards Badrinath and Hemkunt. He has given the details in his book about the trip, how they moved, how much distance they covered in a day, the difficulties and hardships they experienced and some interesting experiences.

They were ten strongwilled men, in love with the mountains and inspired by an awesome mission. They reached Nand Prayag. The local people were surprised to see so many Sikhs together. Local journalists started wondering about their mission, as there was no religious place of the Sikhs on this route. When the journalists persistently asked about the aim of the visit, they informed them about the search of Hemkunt (the Tapasthan of Guru Gobind Singh in his previous life,) and that became headline news in the local newspapers.

First they went to Badrinath went to see Vasudhara waterfalls. Here they met a group of sadhus and among them one was from Punjab. He was also surprised to see so many Sikhs together. These sadhus were returning from a holy trip to Kailash Mansarovar. The Punjabi sadhu asked the Sikh jatha what had brought them there. Partap Singh told the sadhu that they have come in search of a place called Hemkunt.

The sadhu asked him which Hemkunt? Partap Singh was surprised and asked whether there were more than one Hemkunt in this area. The sadhu replied that there is a Hemkunt on the way to Kailash Mansarovar, called Satopath (Satopath is actually the source and origin of Akakhnanda river). It seems that any peak covered with snow is called Hemkunt in this area. Partap Singh was also under the impression that Hemkunt means a mountain covered with snow.

Confused by the sadhu, they were in two minds whether to proceed further or turn back. The team decided that they must visit the place as indicated by Tara Har Narotam and further explained in detail by Sant Sohan Singh. After staying one day at Badrinath, they reached Pandukeshwar the next day.

They rested for the night and started early next morning for Hemkunt. After about six miles, they reached the village Bhionder (It is said that Bhim had performed tapaysa in this village, so the name of the village) and found that all the villagers had gathered to receive them. Normally no outsider visited them and they were surprised to see such a large gathering of the Sikhs. On questioning them, whether there is a place called Hemkunt in this area, one elderly man replied in broken Hindi that there is a small lake at a place called Lokpal. It could be Hemkunt but he was not sure about it. The elderly man, who was a very simple man said that one Sikh Sant who gave his name as Sohan Singh had recently come to this area in search of Hemkunt. The old man also said that Sohan Singh told them that if it is confirmed that Lokpal or Hemkunt is one and the same place, then like Badrinath, this will become a pilgrimage route and you all will be benefitted from it. The old man warned them that the route was very tough.

They moved farther after collecting rations from them and spent a night on the way in the jungle. It was extremely cold and nobody could sleep due to the fast blowing and biting cold winds. At dawn, the coolies accompanying them collected some firewood and lit a fire. After sitting near it for some time they felt comfortable to some extent. The coolies said that the place was only three miles away from there. As the team was used to the plains they thought that three miles would take them only one to two hours to reach the place, so they sent the coolies back to Pandukeshwar telling them that they would return by the evening. But when they resumed their journey, they found that there was no regular path. They had to follow the path carved by the flow of rainwater. It was a very tough ascent and they had to climb holding onto bushes and resting after every few steps. They were exhausted in no time. Though they kept on moving slowly there seemed to be no end. One elderly man refused to move due to total exhaustion but after a lot of a persuasion by the team, he collected some courage and started climbing again.

Just then, they saw a man coming down from a distance. When he came nearer, Sardar Partap Singh recognized that he was Sant Sohan Singh. Pleased to meet a known person in this unfamiliar and secluded place, all of them heaved a sigh of relief. Sant Ji had no prior information about the party but the terrain is such that he being on a higher place could see them coming up. They regained confidence to carry on, but when he told them that they had covered only one mile, their morale sank. After a great deal of encouragement from Sant ji, they started moving slowly, and managed to reach Hemkunt in the afternoon. The first thing they did in Hemkunt was to take a dip in the holy lake and then they sat together to say the daily prayers (Nitnem). They found a small temple near the outlet of the lake. It was cloudy when they reached, but the sky cleared after some time. By this time Sant Sohan Singh also reached, bringing the rear guard with him.

Partap Singh has further written in his book, "Hemkunt as described by Guru Gobind Singh in *Bachitar Natak* must have seven peaks:

Hemkunt parbat hai jahan, sapat sring sobhat hai tahan 11
Sapat Sring teh naam kahawa, panduraj jeh jog kamawa 11

Thus the first indication was that there should be seven peaks. When they started counting the peaks, they found them to be more than seven. They asked Sant ji to show them the seven peaks but he also got confused as the place was suddenly enveloped in clouds. Sometimes he could count four peaks and sometimes he could see eight of them. He said that due to the cloud, he was confused. They were not convinced, but decided to keep quiet as they had come to make a report and not get involved in a discussion.

In *Bachitar Natak*, it is claimed 'Pandu raj jeh jog kamawa.'

So they were looking for the spot where Panduraj had meditated. And according to *Mahabharat*, Panduraj did tapaysa at Ghori Parbat and Kuntikund was near to it. When they enquired about the place, the Sant pointed towards Nanda Parbat. The height of the Parbat as per the Survey Of India map (which they were carrying with them) is 22,000 feet. Not to talk of tapaysa, it was difficult to reach there and survive. When they showed him the survey map and pointed out Ghori Parbat on the map, the Sant got totally confused. He told them he would carry out more research and would duly inform them about it.

Partap Singh goes on to say that as a lot of publicity was given to the place, and funds had started flowing in, so nobody had the time to do further research

After returning to Amritsar, the team met Bhai Vir Singh and submitted the report. Bhai Vir Singh did not waste time in further discussions. He looked at it from a broader perspective. He cherished the vision of seeing his community taking a trip to the beautiful mountains. He said, "If some Sant wants to build a gurudwara at Hemkunt in the mountains, let him do so. Because of this gurudwara, Sikhs will get a Dham like Badrinath in the mountains. Moreover it will be a good excuse for the Sikhs to go to the mountains."

Time has proved him right. A beautiful gurudwara has come up at Hemkunt and lakhs of followers of the Sikh faith visit this place every year to pay their respect. Hemkunt Sahib has given an opportunity to the Sikhs to venture into the mountains. Bhai Vir Singh's poetic vision has made this place famous in the world.

PANDIT TARA HAR NAROTAM

In the Sikh circles he is known as Pandit Tara Singh Narotam but he calls himself Pandit Tara Har Narotam as indicated in his book *Gur Tirath Sangrah.* He was born in 1823 AD in village Kalman in district Gurdaspur (Punjab). There is no record available about his parents and early life. Though he belonged to an agriculturist family, he had religious leanings as he used to spend most of his time in the company of sadhus. He gained vast knowledge by reading old religious books and granths. Seeing his bent of mind, somebody advised him to search for a guru under whose guidance he could do more studies. Ultimately somebody told him about Pandit Gulab Singh who used to stay with his followers in village Kurala in district Hoshiarpur and he reached there. At that time he was barely 20 years old. He served under Pandit Gulab Singh sincerely and became a Nirmala Sadhu. With his guru's blessing, he went to Amritsar for further studies. From here he went to Kashi, Benaras, and spent some time reading Vedas, Vidang, Khat Darshan Dharam Shastra. In the meantime, in 1918, the festival of Ardh Kumbh (half kumbh) was to be celebrated at Hardwar and he reached there. He met many learned people there and had discussions with them earning a name for himself. People from far and near started coming to him to hear

his sermons. Maharaja Narinder Singh of Patiala heard about him and he requested him to come and stay in his estate and help him in all respects. Here he wrote many books and granths such as *Japji Teeka, Rahras Teeka, Sohila Teeka, Shabad Hazare Teeka, Bhagat Banis Teeka, Gurmit Nirney Sagar, Guru Granth Kosh, Sri Rag Teeka,* etc.

He took interest in religious places of the Sikhs associated with the Sikh gurus. He visited all the places and published *Gur Tirath Sangrah* in 1884 in which he described 508 gurudwaras or places connected with the gurus. After reading about Guru Gobind Singh's past life in *Bachitar Natak* he identified the exact spot which was the Guru's Tap Sathan and described it (pp. 86 to 97).

Because of his original research, there is a gurudwara in Hemkunt and thousands of devotees visit it and take the Guru's blessings. No details are known about how he reached there and how he found the place or what difficulties and problems he must have encountered – the sketch map he made is very accurate.

BHAI VIR SINGH

Today's Punjabi literature period is called Bhai Vir Singh's era and it is absolutely correct. Literary historians today trace to him the origin of Punjabi prose, novel, lyric, epic, drama and historical research. From his pen flowed great novels, poetry, drama, epic, exegesis, biography, juvenile literature and essays.

Bhai Vir Singh was born on 5 December 1872 in Amritsar. His ancestor Bhai Kaura Mal (died 1752) was the prime minister to the governor of Lahore and was a friend of the Sikhs. By his tact, he helped Sikhs in difficult times. Bhai Vir Singh's father, Sardar Charan Singh, was an ayurvedic doctor and was proficient in Sanskrit, Braj, English and Persian besides Punjabi. Vir Singh was the eldest of Dr Charan Singh's family of six children. He completed recitation of Guru Granth Sahib when he was eight years old. He studied Persian, Urdu and Sanskrit. At the age of nineteen, he took his matriculation examination topping the list and wining a gold medal. Though he could have joined the government service, he preferred to become a divinity teacher in Khalsa School, Amritsar. He was a deeply religious man and dedicated himself to serving Singh Sabha. In 1892 A.D, in collaboration with his friend Wazir Singh he established a lithograph press in Amritsar. It was called Wazir-e-Hind press after the name of his partner, as he himself wanted to remain in anonymity. The following year, he started Khalsa Tract Society and started a weekly newspaper called Khalsa Samachar. The first issue of the paper was brought out in 1899.

He became famous by writing the great novel called *Sundri*, the first novel of Punjabi language, which was published in 1898. It gained immediate popularity and caught the imagination of the Sikhs. Since its first publication, it has gone into 34 editions, totaling a million copies. He wrote many more novels such as *Bijay Singh*, *Satwant Kaur* and *Baba Naudh Singh*.

He was at home with poetry as well as prose. He wrote

Rana Surat Singh, an epic with more than twelve thousand lines. He wrote only one play called *Raja Lakhdata Singh*, which was published in 1910. He wrote many poetry books: *Trel Trupke, Lehran De Har, Bijlian De Har, Mutak Hulare* and many more. His short poems show depth of feeling and are mature in content and style. His poems reflect the poet's inner feeling. He will be remembered for his scholarly work. The first one he chose for scholarly scrutiny was *Sikhan Di Bhagat Mala* by Bhai Mani Singh (1644-1734) and published in 1912. He also edited and published for the first time the celebrated *Prachin Panth Parkash*. He edited *Puratan Janamsakhi*, which to this date is the most reliable and valuable source material on the life of Guru Nanak Dev. As mentioned in the text, he undertook to edit *Gur Partap Suraj Granth* by Bhai Santokh Singh. For nine years, he was completely busy with this monumental work and it was published in 1934 in 14 volumes. He has published *Sri Kaligidhar Chamatkar* (two volumes, 1925), followed by *Sri Guru Nanak Chamatkar* (two volumes, 1928) giving life stories of Guru Gobind Singh and Guru Nanak respectively and also *Ashat Gur Chamatkar* giving life sketches of the second to the ninth guru.

East Punjab University honoured him by conferring the degree of Doctor of Oriental Languages in 1949. He was nominated a member of Punjab Legislative Council. In 1953 he received the Sahiyta Academy award for his book *Mere Saiyan Jeeo*. On 6 October 1956 the President of India conferred on him the Padma Bhushan. His end came on 10 June 1957.

"Bhai Vir Singh Sadan" has been constructed near Gol Market in New Delhi in his memory and a lot of research work is being done. His writings in *Kalgidhar Chamatkar* led Sant Sohan Singh of Tehri (Garhwal) to search for Hemkunt Parbat, after Tara Singh Narotam. Bhai Vir Singh helped him a lot in setting up a 10'x10' gurudwara as well as motivated the Sikh Sangat to visit Hemkunt and have darshan. The first jatha, that went to Hemkunt in 1952, was motivated by him. Master Karam Singh organised and led the jatha after reading Bhai Vir Singh's writings.

HAVILDAR BABA MODAN SINGH JI

Havildar Baba Modan Singh was born in a small village called Lakhanpur in district Ludhiana (Punjab). At a young age he

joined the Indian Army and was allotted Bengal Sappers, whose main function is to help lay roads, build bridges, etc. With his good behaviour and hard work, he reached the rank of havildar, which was considered a big rank by Indians in those days. After retirement he joined the Survey of India and was posted in Mussoorie as a civilian.

By chance, when Sant Sohan Singh was collecting material for the small gurudwara to be built at Hemkunt, he met Havildar Modan Singh in a shop in Mussoorie. As both men had retired from the army, they soon struck up a friendship. When Havildar Modan

Singh asked him what he was doing Sant Sohan Singh explained his mission. Havildar Modan Singh got interested in his mission and offered his services whenever required. He went with him to Hemkunt and helped him in building the gurudwara. By the untimely death of Sant Sohan Singh in 1939, the unfinished task of construction was left in the hands of Havildar Modan Singh, as he was well aware of the work involved and understood the importance of it. Other devotees gradually joined him and the work progressed.

At that time there was no place to stay at Gobind Dham (Ghagria as it was then known). He used to spend the night in the hollow of a tree trunk. He built a dharamshala at Gobind Ghat and Gobind Dham for the pilgrims. Since the workload increased, it was difficult for him to manage all alone so he set up a trust in 1960 but unfortunately he did not live long and left for his heavenly abode shortly afterwards, in his native place. Due to his hard work, Hemkunt became famous and devotees started coming in large numbers from all over the world. Since he had laid a strong foundation and had done the right planning, so the trust did not find any difficulty in carrying out the mission. It was just due to his hard work, and his unflinching devotion, honesty and Sewa Bhav (selfless service), that he is remembered in the Sikh world.

It is again a pity that not much is known about him. No one has thought of writing a book on him. With the passage of time only a threadbare outline of his life and work will be known and all the hard work he had undertaken will be forgotten. Hemkunt Trust should take up this task immediately.

BHAI NANDA SINGH CHUHAN

Nanda Singh Chuhan hails from a village called Bhiondar, about 8 km from Gobind Ghat enroute to Hemkunt. His father Rattan Singh Chuhan was the headman of this village. His family has been associated with Hemkunt since 1934, when Sant Sohan Singh came here in search of this place and stayed with Rattan Singh who helped him in reaching Hemkunt. Nanda Singh was born in 1914. Though he is 88 years old now, he is still active and has a good memory. He narrates the stories of the past to the yatris and can narrate all the events from the discovery of Hemkunt, to the coming up of the new Gurudwara. He has written a small book called *Sri Hemkunt Sahib – Tap Asthan Darshan* in Punjabi, which is published by Bhai Chhater Singh Jiwan Singh, Amritsar in which he has given all the events.

He helped in the construction of the 10'x10' gurudwara, and was appointed as its caretaker on a salary of Rs 12/- per annum. Though he did not know Gurmukhi he was taught to perform all the rituals. Later on he learnt Gurmukhi from Sant Thandi Singh and could recite *Guru Granth Sahib*.

When *Guru Granth Sahib* was to be taken to Hemkunt, for the first time, he volunteered to take the *Granth Sahib* on his head, as per the traditions. He helped in the purchase of land for a dharamshala at Gobind Ghat. Whenever any work was to be carried out, he used to take the contract and complete the work to the satisfaction of every one. When the pathway was to be laid between Gobind Dham and Hemkunt, there was no one to guide, as no survey was carried out and there were no engineers. He volunteered to do the job and did it remarkably well. There has been no change in it since it was built in 1954 and lakhs of yatris have trekked on it.

When the hazardous task of installing Nishan Sahibs on the seven hills was proposed he, along with Sant Surat Singh, accepted the challenge and completed the seemingly impossible task.

He did not have a son. Havildar Modan Singh did ardas for him and he was blessed with a son named Bhagat Singh. Later on he got two more sons.

As per his book, he was employed at the salary of Rs 12 per annum in 1936 and this continued up to 1940 when it was increased to Rs 18 per year. In1954, Sant Thandi Singh increased this to Rs 60. After the formation of the Trust, his pay was fixed at Rs 50 per month. He retired in 1975 due to old age though he was again called in 1984. He refused to accept the pension of a ridiculously small amount after retirement. He lives on the charity of yatris only.

He is the oldest man living among those who were associated with the Hemkunt Gurudwara from the very inception, i.e. 1934, but it is a pity that public is not aware of him and just pass by his village without even noticing this village. It is suggested that some sort of memorial should be erected firstly in the name of Bhiondar village, which did a lot of work in the initial stages by helping the yatris to undertake the rough yatra and the second memorial should be built in the name of Nanda Singh. His memoirs should be recorded and kept in some library as a source of inspiration for future generations of devotees and scholars.

the first gurudwara

Jithe Baba paer dharey puja aasan thaapan soha

After considering all the factors including the opinion of S. Partap Singh, Bhai Vir Singh decided to build a gurudwara, and deputed Sant Sohan Singh for the job. He chose the place that had been identified by him. Bhai Vir Singh

View of first 10" x 10" Gurudwara which was constructed in 1936 at the height of 15,200 feet.

considered the following factors before giving the final approval:

1 Material for the construction of gurudwara was not available locally.
2 Material to be purchased from Rishikesh, the nearest city situated at a distance of 300 kms.
3 Transportation of the construction material, including over the last 18 km where no path exists.
4 Estimated cost of the construction.
5 Source of the funds.
6 Management of the gurudwara after its completion.
7 Will the devotees visit that place in spite of the hazardous route and difficulties on the way?

It took approximately one month for Bhai Vir Singh to consider all the factors and formulate his plans. Then he called Sant Sohan Singh and gave him his approval and suggested that he should go there and start the work. 'Wahe Guru will look after the problems if any and solve them,' he told him. As for the management of the gurudwara, Bhai Vir Singh thought of asking the Mussoorie Gurudwara to look after it. But he was not aware how far Hemkunt is from Mussoorie and how difficult it would be for the management to look after it from such a distance. Alternatively he considered the possibility of handing over the responsibility to Chief Khalsa Diwan, Amritsar.

It was decided that a gurudwara of the size of 10'x10' with a verandah of three feet in front of it be constructed around the shila where Guru Gobind Singh did tapaysa in his previous birth and Parkash (placing) of the *Guru Granth Sahib* should be done at the exact spot. Bhai Vir Singh donated Rs 500 from his pocket for the noble cause and decided that on hearing from Sant Sohan Singh, he would send more money to Rishikesh at the address provided by him.

By the time the final decision was taken for the construction of the gurudwara at Hemkunt, winter had set in, so it was decided to take up the construction work during the next summer when the snow would have melted and all the routes would be open. Bhai Vir Singh purchased all the items connected with the gurudwara (Guru Granth Sahib, Bir, romala, etc.), books, a small tent and gave it to Sant Sohan Singh. After detailed discussions, in which the work was explained, Sant ji left for Tehri.

Next year Sant Sohan Singh went to Mussoorie in connection with some work, and met Havildar Modan Singh in a shop, by chance. Havildar Modan Singh introduced himself to Sant ji and asked him what he was doing in Mussoorie. Sant ji explained in detail the project he had undertaken. Havildar Modan Singh got interested and requested to be associated with the project.

A view of the First Gurudwara and the snow peaks

Sant Sohan Singh gladly accepted his offer. The saying goes that one plus one becomes eleven, the two of them were now a team.

In August 1936 Sant Sohan Singh wrote a letter to Bhai Vir Singh asking for necessary funds and Bhai Vir Singh sent it by telegraphic money order at the given address in Rishikesh. Sant Ji purchased all the necessary material, loaded it on the mules and started for Hemkunt. He reached Bhiondar village and stayed with Rattan Singh Chuhan, the headman of the village. They called Hyat Singh who was a contractor at Badrinath and explained the whole project to him. After deciding upon the rates, the contract was awarded to him. When the locals came to know that Sikhs were building a gurudwara at their place, they objected to it. It is said that the locals threw the shila on which Guru Gobind Singh had done tapasya in the lake. Sant Sohan Singh explained to them that a gurudwara is the abode of God and their place of worship will not be disturbed, but they did not agree and made a lot of hue and cry. Ultimately it was decided that a temple of the size of 6'x 6' would also be constructed by its side, simultaneously. Then they agreed to allow the construction of the gurudwara. Hyat Singh started work on the gurudwara and the temple. Sant Sohan Singh wrote to Havildar Modan Singh asking him to send a steel pole of 10' length, so that Nishan Sahib could be hoisted. Havildar Modan Singh brought the necessary material and after staying for a few days, returned to Mussoorie.

Sant Ji stayed at the place of construction for two months and got all the work completed. After the work was completed Karah Parsad was prepared and distributed among the locals, and they were very happy. When they had done their job and were satisfied in all respects, they locked the building of the gurudwara and left for Joshimath. After checking all the accounts, payment was made to Hyat Singh. It was noticed that more than twice the amount estimated was spent. But, at no stage, was there any shortage of funds.

In August 1937, it was decided that *Guru Granth Sahib* should be installed in the Gurudwara. Sant Sohan Singh carried the *Guru Granth Sahib* on his head all the way to Bhiondar. He also took with him all the other accessories, which were given by Bhai Vir Singh in 1935. He reached the village Bhiondar and stayed in the house of Rattan Singh Chuhan. From Bhiondar, it was Nanda Singh, son of Rattan Singh, who was a young boy, who volunteered to do this job. It was a very difficult job as it involved locking of the hands around the Beed on the head and climbing in the hostile terrain. But Nanda Singh performed the job to the complete satisfaction of everyone and Guru Granth Sahib's Beed was installed in the Gurudwara as per the traditions. Langar was cooked in the village and carried to the gurudwara. It was served to the locals who were very happy.

Later on, he felt the need of a dharamshala at Ghagria and got a tin shed constructed so that yatris could spend a night with out any problem.

At last Sant Sohan Singh's wishes were fulfilled. He wanted to have a gurudwara at Hemkunt and it was constructed under his supervision. He never knew that this was his last visit to the place he had discovered. After returning from Hemkunt, he fell ill and died on 13 February 1939. It seems that God had entrusted to him the job of construction of the gurudwara at the holy place and installing of the *Guru Granth Sahib*. When the job was completed, He called him back as if his services were no longer required on the earth. Sant Sohan Singh had probably been suffering from tuberculosis for quite a while but had not told anyone about it. Staying continuously at a great height his health had deteriorated.

Before returning to Amritsar Sant Sohan Singh had explained all the chores to be done pertaining to the service and upkeep of the gurudwara to Nanda Singh. The latter did not know Gurmukhi, but was taught how to do parkash, prepare karah parsad and keep the gurudwara clean. So officially Nanda Singh was the first Sewadar, the first Granthi of the Hemkunt Gurudwara and he performed the duties of the caretaker of the gurudwara up to 1975 religiously and to the satisfaction of all concerned. It is heard that Sant Thandi Singh helped him in learning Gurmukhi language and also taught him how to recite Guru Granth Sahib.

DEATH OF SANT SOHAN SINGH

He was further working to improve the conditions at Ghagria, when he found that his tuberculosis had aggravated. He reached Amrirsar and reported to Bhai Vir Singh who had him admitted to the hospital. Though he got good treatment, he did not recover and after staying for a month in the hospital, he died on 13th February 1939. Bhai Vir Singh looked after him and bore all the expenses incurred on his treatment. He was cremated and again all the expenses were borne by Bhai Vir Singh. Bhog ceremony including Akhand Path was held in Central Khalsa Yatim Khana.

After Sant Sohan Singh's death Havildar Modan Singh took over the job of looking after the work and further improving it. He used to visit Hemkunt every year and change the chola of Nishan Sahib

Sant Sohan Singh used to narrate a story that when he was busy constructing the gurudwara, he often met a sadhu who was very old and used to stay naked and had grey hair all over his body. Locals also confirmed that a sadhu keeps on roaming in this place but he never talks with anybody. If some body wished him he would just raise his hand and give his blessings. Once he came to Sant Sohan Singh and he wished him. The Sadhu gave him his blessings by raising his hand and said that you are doing a wonderful job. It was at the same place where Guru Ji used to do tapasya. After that he was not seen again.

FIRST AKHAND PATH AT HEMKUNT

Dr Tara Singh of Nahan met Havildar Modan Singh in August 1946 for the first time when he was preparing for a visit to Hemkunt. Dr Tara Singh decided to accompany Havildar Modan Singh as the latter was getting ready for his next trip to Hemkunt. One of the relatives of Havildar Modan Singh and one more Sant who belonged to Ludhiana decided to accompany them. All the four walked together from Rishikesh. On the way they decided that this time they must do Akhand Path at the holy place. They bought all the essential items, especially ghee, to provide light by burning in an earthen lamp. From Bhiondar, they took a local man for guidance. They started the Akhand

Path as per the traditions. They found out that only two persons were able to recite the path – Dr Tara Singh and the Sant from Ludhiana. They decided to sit for two hours at a time and then change the duty. Havildar Modan Singh took the most difficult task of keeping the diya (earthen pot for light) burning because ghee used to freeze at such a high altitude due to cold. One had to keep on burning the coal beneath the diya, so that enough heat was provided for the ghee to melt and for the wick to keep on burning. The fourth man took over the kitchen duty – to provide tea and food. On the second day ardas was performed at Madh (half way). On the third day at the end of the path, they performed kirtan and sounded jaikara of 'Bole So Nihal – Sat Sri Akal.' The whole valley reverberated with the sound. Thus these four men with strong will power, performed the first Akhand Path at Hemkunt Sahib at such a high altitude. Karah Prasad was prepared and distributed. Then they closed the gurudwara and came back.

Earlier a group of students from Amritsar had gone and done kirtan in the Hemkunt gurudwara.

1946 ONWARDS

Reaching Hemkunt was still a Herculean task but a few determined devotees started taking up the challenge to pay homage to the place made holy by their Guru. Off and on, a few people could be seen on those otherwise lonely places. In 1950, the road was constructed up to Chamoli. One could travel in the bus up to Chamoli but the onward distance was to be covered on foot.

So far Bhai Vir Singh looked after all the work of the gurudwara but in 1951 he had discussions with the management of Chief Khalsa Diwan Amritsar and handed over all the responsibilities to them. He published an appeal in *Khalsa Samachar* dated 25th September 1952 and asked the public to donate money liberally so that this Gurudwara could be managed properly. It was further said that an amount of Rs one lakh should be deposited with Chief Khalsa Diwan so that with its interest the gurudwara could be managed. The public responded to the appeal and the amount started coming to Chief Khalsa Diwan for which a separate bank account was opened. The complete responsibility was given to Bhai Karam Singh who was Superintendent Central Khalsa Yatim Khana under the auspices of Chief Khalsa Diwan, to manage Hemkunt and other places connected with it. He submitted a report on 30 June 1953, that the following amount had been received and deposited in Punjab and Sindh Bank at Rishikesh:

A For one lakh Golak appeal – Rs 14,321 and 12 annas have been revceived.

B For the construction of new Gurudwara at Gobind Dham – Rs 2,307.

C For the path from Ghagria to Hemkunt – Rs 5,229.

D Running account for managing the gurudwara – Rs 6,100.00

Bhai Vir Singh persuaded Master Karam Singh to take jathas to Hemkunt. In 1951, Master Karam Singh went alone on 3 September 1951 and returned on 18th September after fifteen days of reconnoitring the area. He reached Hemkunt on

10 September and spent the night there.

He led the first official jatha in 1952. Twenty-eight persons, including four ladies were part of this jatha which started from Amritsar. One person named Bhai Uttam Singh ji was a Surma Singh Ragi (blind preacher). They purchased their rations from Rishikesh. Sixteen coolies were engaged to carry the luggage (each coolie could carry one maund of luggage at the rate of Rs 60). Six persons joined the group at Rishikesh. Total strength of the jatha was thirty-four. On 26th August they left Rishikesh but found that the river Chanderbhaga was in spate so they crossed it with great difficulty either on horses or on foot and boarded the buses. When they reached Lakshman Jhoola they found that the road was washed away so they had to wait for four hours till the road was repaired. They had to spend the night at Dev Prayag. Again they found that the road was washed away and they had to walk. With great difficulty the jatha reached Srinagar (Garhwal) at 1430 hours. S. Harnam Singh Siali joined them here so the strength of the jatha rose to thirty-five. Now they were twenty-nine men and six women. Next day they left for Chamoli. From here they started walking on foot with Baba Modan Singh leading with *Guru Granth Sahib* on his head. They stopped at Shen Chatti and on the second day reached Pipalkoti. On 31 August, the jatha reached Joshimath and spent the night at the residence of Seth Kaloo Ram Shah who held Baba Modan Singh in great respect. Joshimath was decorated with flags and buntings and the jatha was treated as celebrities. In the evening, all the prominent persons of Joshimath attended the Kirtan.

On 1 September the jatha reached Gobind Ghat and many more yatris joined the jatha. Guru Granth Sahib was installed in the newly built dharamshala with proper Sikh traditions. The jatha left on 4 September for Hemkunt and reached at 1430 hours with the help of villagers from Bhiondar. They took the ritual bath in the sarovar, and did non-stop kirtan in the night. The jatha returned to Gobind Ghat on 6 September and reached Hardwar from where they took the train to Amritsar on the same day – 16 September. It took them 25 days to complete this historic yatra. These details have been provided by Chief Khalsa Diwan Amtitsar.

Since there was no path, it was decided that the goverenment should be approached to carry out the survey for the path which they thought would be done free of cost. Anyhow they started collecting money for the construction of the road. Rs 610 were collected on the spot and the yatris promised to give an additional amount of Rs 2895. An account was opened in Punjab and Sindh Bank, Rishikesh, for the construction of the road.

Master Karam Singh took four more jathas consisting of more than hundred yatris during the next four years i.e. up to 1956. Sant Thandi Singh joined the jatha in 1953 and after visiting Hemkunt, he was so impressed that he decided to stay there for Sewa (selfless service) and did a lot of work. The people of Bhiondar village were of great help too. All the jathas used to take the local people who helped them in negotiating the climb. At some stage, one villager used to help two to three yatris in reaching Hemkunt. Because there were no regular paths the yatris, particularly from the plains, faced a lot of problems.

In 1953, Master Karam Singh gave an ultimatum to Baba

Modan Singh, that if by the next year no regular path was constructed, he would not bring any jatha. Ultimately, Havildar Modan Singh called the contractor Hyat Singh and after discussion gave him a contract to lay down the path from Ghagria to Hemkunt at the rate of Rs 200 for a furlong (8 furlongs make a mile or 1.6 km). The total distance was little more than 3 miles and the estimated cost was Rs 5,000 only. But no one knew where and how to lay down the path as no survey had been carried out and they had no engineers at hand. Baba Modan Singh also got worried when this problem was given to him. He called Nanda Singh and asked for his advice. Ultimately it was Nanda Singh who guided the contractor. Not that he had any technical know-how, but because he had traversed the path many times and knew it like the back of his hand.

He suggested a new route. Earlier they used to cross the river Hem Ganga at Ghagria itself and then go up directly. The construction work on the route from Ghagria to Hemkunt was started on 23 May 1953 and was completed by the end of September. It has got 65 sharp bends. This path still exists and no changes have been made. Next year when Master Karam Singh brought a jatha all the yatris reached Hemkunt without any assistance. The same pathway has been used by lakhs of devotees but no body has thought of improving it.

When Nanda Singh was asked how he decided to construct this path, where no survey was carried out, he said that he was just guided by some spiritual power.

In 1955, Dr Tara Singh decided to spend a few days at Hemkunt all alone. He travelled from Chamoli on a bicycle. In those days no villagers or local people had seen a bicycle and it caused quite a stir. He reached Gobind Ghat and was told that Hemkunt was covered with snow so he went back. He again came in May and met a Sant at Gobind Ghat. They travelled together to Hemkunt and found that the gurudwara was covered with three feet of snow. After clearing the snow, they opened the lock and, to their surprise, they found that the gurudwara was absolutely dry from inside but rats had made their holes in it. They spent the night in the temple premises. The Sant came down next day. Dr. Tara Singh used to get up early in the morning, and after taking a bath in the lake, he used to recite the Nitnem and Sukhmani. Later in the morning he would recite the Path from *Guru Granth Sahib*. He spent two-and-a-half months all alone there. He has written his experiences in his book called *Hemkunt Darshan*. All the locals were surprised to see a human being spend such a long time at such a height all alone. It happens by the grace of Gurus only.

In 1957, Bhai Vir Singh died. It was a big blow to the Hemkunt project, because in case of any problem they used to approach him and he used to give the correct advice. It was only with his guidance and monetary help that Hemkunt had come into existence and was known to people who started travelling in large numbers. No work was taken up without consulting him. Havildar Modan Singh felt orphaned. Without Bhai Vir Singh there was no one to guide him and inspire him. But with experience and dedication he managed to take control of the situation and worked with more zeal.

Havildar Modan Singh also narrated that he often saw a certain Jogi in Vasudhara next to Badrinath. He was a naked saint, and would remain naked even in the snow. He was usually seen in

Samadhi. People would keep food next to him but he never ate it and never wore any clothes even in extreme winter. Havildar Modan Singh had many talks with him when he was not in Samadhi. He would tell him old stories connected with those places. He was well versed with the topography of that area. Even he confirmed that the Guru had done tapasya at Hemkunt. He was very happy that a gurudwara was being constructed to immortalise the holy spot. He was always blessing the persons involved in the task.

NISHAN SAHIB ON THE SEVEN PEAKS

Major Umrao Singh Bains played a significant role in spreading the word about the importance of Hemkunt. In his book he has written that the gurudwara at Joshimath and Ghagria were constructed under the supervision of Sant Thandi Singh. Major Bains used to visit various gurudwaras in different cities of India when possible and at the end of Diwan, with the permission of authorities, used to speak about the importance of Hemkunt and persuade the people to take the yatra. Later on he started taking yatris in buses and provided lots of material for the langar. He carried on this work till his demise in 1999. And now, a dedicated team of people whom he had trained, continue the good work.

In Rishikesh, Bhai Surat Singh, a carpenter by profession, received inspiration from Guru Gobind Singh, while he was meditating one day, to install Nishan Sahib on all the seven peaks surrounding the lake. In 1960, he motivated Nanda Singh who helped him to install a Nishan Sahib on the fourth peak, which is the main and highest peak. He was carrying with him a Nishan Sahib mounted on a three foot wooden pole. Nanda Singh told him that the approach to the fourth peak was very difficult but he insisted on doing the job. So early one morning both of them left for the fourth peak with the wooden Nishan Sahib. The going was very tough but helping each other, with great difficulty they reached there and managed to install the Nishan Sahib. It was a very daring feat indeed. Next year, he brought three steel pipes of the length of eight feet. They hired a villager to carry one of the pipes and the other two pipes they carried themselves. Again helping each other they managed to reach the top without any mishap. The pipes were assembled there and a permanent Nishan Sahib was hoisted at the highest peak (it is probably the highest Nishan Sahib in the world). In 1962 they went round the remaining six peaks and firstly installed wooden Nishan Sahibs. The idea was to see the route and get to know the difficulties on the way. In subsequent years they were changed to steel poles. Every year in the month of August/September the cholas of all the seven Nishan Sahibs are changed. A team of dedicated persons from Sabo ki Talwandi (Bhatinda) has kept up the tradition. Some other young yatris also take up this challenge and perform this sewa. May Wahe Guru give them enough courage and zeal to continue with such a challenging task.

HEMKUNT TRUST

With Bhai Vir Sngh gone, Havildar Modan Singh was finding it very difficult to shoulder such a heavy responsibility. Lots of people advised him to make a trust. The first meeting was held at the residence of Col Joginder Singh Maan who was a minister in PEPSU state and a draft for the trust was prepared. A prominent lawyer was consulted in Chandigarh and he amended the draft considering all the legal points. He advised that since the deed had to be registered in U.P. this draft should be shown to some lawyer in Uttar Pradesh as rules for all the states are different. A prominent lawyer in Kanpur was consulted and he amended it. This trust was named Gurudwara Shri Hemkunt Management Trust and was registered in 1960. There were seven members in the trust who were dedicated men. The following were elected as members:

1 Havildar Baba Modan Singh (President)
2 Lt Col Joginder Singh Maan
3 S. Gurmakh Singh, Ludhiana
4 S. Raghbir Singh, Delhi
5 S. Shamsher Singh, Kanpur
6 S. Gurbakash Singh Bindra, Rishikesh
7 Colonel Amar Singh, Amritsar.

Lt Col Joginder Singh Maan was nominated as Secretary. The permanent address of this trust is in Kanpur.

Havildar Baba Modan Singh called a meeting of the Trust in October 1960 at Rishkesh. All the members assembled in Delhi at the residence of S.Raghbir Singh and requested Baba ji to come there. He got annoyed and ordered them to come to Rishikesh. Next morning all of them reached Rishikesh where the meeting was held. Baba Ji said that he did not want to shoulder the responsibilities any more and put the keys on the table. He further said that they must continue to serve the yatris and try to improve the conditions of their stay at various places in spite of the opposition from a section of people. The members thought that he was angry with them as they had not come directly to Rishikesh so they tried to persuade him to carry on. But he declined to take the responsibility. After the meeting he left for Ludhiana and died peacefully on 25 December 1960, on the birthday of Guru Gobind Singh. It again looked as if Wahe Guru was waiting for him to fulfill the mission before calling him back.

the present gurudwara

Its Proposal, Design and Construction

A small gurudwara, 10'x10' with a three foot verendah in front was constructed using local material in 1934-36 at the place, identified as Hemkunt where, according to *Bachitar Natak*, Guru Gobind Singh Ji, did tapasya in his previous life. Shri *Guru Granth Sahib* was installed in this gurudwara and Nishan Sahib was hoisted as is the tradition of Sikh maryada. Slowly and steadily people started visiting this place and with Bhai Vir Singh's writings more and more devotees started coming to pay their homage. With the passage of time, when it was seen that this place was too small to accommodate the increasing number of devotees, the necessity of a bigger gurudwara was felt.

In 1960 a lady, Mai Ram Kaur, hailing from Mirzapur in Uttar Pradesh, accompanied a jatha from Kanpur for a visit to this holy place. At the end of the Diwan at Gobind Ghat she got up and with due permission narrated her own story. She said, "I was not aware of any place called Hemkunt Sahib in India or any other part of the world as nobody ever talked to me about it." She recounted that about four months earlier, in 1959, when she was praying, she got a vision in which Guru Gobind Singh appeared and directed her that a very big and magnificent gurudwara should be built on the place where he did tapasya in his previous birth. On enquiry, she found out the whereabouts of Hemkunt. When she heard of a jatha going from Kanpur to Hemkunt Sahib, she decided to join the jatha and visit Hemkunt Sahib. She reached Kanpur on the appointed day and joined the jatha which was led by Sardar Shamsher Singh.

On hearing this story, Havildar Baba Modan Singh got up and said that Guru Gobind Singh had ordered him too that a very big and beautiful gurudwarwa should be constructed at the place where he did tapasya in his previous birth. This gurudwara should be the best and should be big enough to accommodate a large gathering. How far the two identical stories are true is anybody's guess but a wave of jubilation spread over the Sangat in which every devotee was carried away. It was taken as the order of the Guru and with his blessings too. Every one wanted to participate in the project and contribute.

It was decided to send for contractor Hyat Singh, who had been associated with the gurudwara since its inception. He was consulted and asked how large a gurudwara could be constructed at such a height. He advised that before taking on such a big project, a temporary shed should be constructed where the material could be stored and the people working on the site could stay. It would also provide a resting place for the yatris, if any, who would be tired after the long and hazardous trek. It was decided to make a temporary shed on the bank of river Hem Ganga. It was estimated that this temporary place consisting of three rooms would cost Rs 21,000.00. Mrs Issar Oberai gladly volunteered to bear this cost and it was accepted by the sangat with traditional jaikara. It was further decided that it should be named after Bhai Vir Singh who had played an important role in this task. And so it was named Bhai Vir Singh Niwas Asthan.

Takht Shri Patna Sahib and Shiromani Gurudwara Prabandhak Committee Amritsar decided that on the auspicious occasion of Shri Guru Gobind Singh's 300th birth anniversary in 1966, the celebrations should start from Hemkunt Sahib. Some members of the Trust reached Hemkunt in early June to make arrangements. Luckily some VIPs such as S.Gurnam Singh, Chief Justice of Punjab High Court, Justice Ranjit Singh Narula, S. Nihal Singh along with 18 members of the management committee came there to pay their homage. Fortunately Major General Harkirat Singh, Engineer-in-Chief, Indain Army along with Brigadier Jarnail Singh Sandhu were also going to pay their homage at the same time. It was a lucky coincidence that S. Joginder Singh Maan, President Hemkunt Trust, S. Shamsher Singh, general secretary, S.Gurbakash Singh, member and Dr. Inderjit Singh, Chairman Punjab and Sindh Bank were also on their way to Hemkunt.

All the above dignitaries met on the way. After the preliminary introductions, the talk about the new gurudwara started and General Harkirat Singh invited them to Joshimath where he was staying. In the evening the entire party reached Joshimath and an important meeting was held in which they were to change the shape of the gurudwara in Hemkunt. General Harkirat Singh said that Hemkunt is a very beautiful place, and a picturesque gurudwara should be built there and it should be so designed that it should surpass all other buildings, both in concept and shape at such a height. If possible it should be the eighth wonder of the world and people from all over the world should come here to pay homage. All those present fully agreed with the concept but regretted that they had neither the technical know–how nor the resources to make it a reality. General Harkirat Singh humbly promised to undertake the task of surveying the area, collecting relevant information and getting the drawings of the basic structure and the complete building. The management committee and others who were present immediately accepted the offer.

Manmohan Singh Siali, who became the architect of the new gurudwara, in his book *Gurudwara in the Himalayas, Hemkunt Sahib* has written that when the Trust decided to build a bigger gurudwara in place of the 10'x10' old gurudwara, the initial design was prepared by S.Beant Singh of Chandigarh. His concept was apparently designed without any knowledge of the site and climatic conditions. When General Harkirat Singh was shown the design by one of the Trust members for an appraisal, he could immediately detect the flaws. He felt that the concept was lacking not only in terms of compatibility of the site and climatic conditions but also in terms of size and capacity. The proposed design, which gave primary consideration to the religious aspect, did not take into account the demands of the extremely difficult site and the climate, by far the most important factors. The heavily contoured site presented major construction constraints like its location in the seismic zone, being prone to snow avalanches and high velocity winds and the presence of Remount lake itself, which should have been the primary factors that governed the design. A man of rare vision, the General felt that with the passage of time the number of pilgrims and visitors would swell manifold. His prediction has come true. He was of the opinion that 400-500 people would be the right number to accommodate in the congregation hall at one time. Agreeing with the General, the trust management committee entrusted him with the responsibility of finding the architect who could accomplish the project keeping in mind all the important factors as pointed by him.

The General selected Manmohan Singh Siali, who was working as an architect in Military Engineering Services (M.E.S.) under him. He felt that Siali, with the experience of handling a multitude of projects and being a devoted Sikh with the knack of imitating architecture for gurudwaras, had the right experience to handle a project of such dimension. However since the architect was working for the M.E.S., he required official permission to take up an independent civil project. The permission was sought and duly accorded.

A team of architects and engineers visited the site in the month of October 1965. The following points were considered:

1 Terrain

2 Climate

3 Level of the lake

4 Soil Type

5 Snow avalanches and slides as snow-laden mountains surrounded the lake.

Snow was also a common factor and thus the constructed building would have to be designed to sustain a certain snow load.

6 Earthquakes, measuring 6.5 to 7.5 on the Richter scale had to be considered, since the location fell in the seismic belt.

7 High velocity winds.

8 Flooding, due to a rise in the level of the water in the lake.

9 Site where the Gurudwara will be built.

From the above, it is seen that without survey, no work could be started. Survey of India was entrusted with this work. The Survey of India prepared the graphs of what was to become the first ever site for survey of an area located at such high altitude. The survey plan revealed that the level of its closely placed contours ranged between 20 to 25 metres. The siting was a very crucial factor not only because the gurudwara had to be guarded against all the climatic hazards but also had to be designed in order to accommodate 400-500 people, which was a substantial number. Besides, the architect was keen to see that the gurudwara be sited in such a way that the people inside could get a view of the picturesque surroundings of the Hemkunt lake. Moreover the initial gurudwara, which marked the tapshila place of the Dusht Daman, had to be preserved in the new design.

DESIGN

While designing the gurudwara, the designers focused on providing a structure that would be able to withstand the elements of nature. In this case the onslaught of snow avalanches and landslides, occurrence of earthquakes, high velocity winds and flooding due to rising level of the lake. They had to keep in view the global warming effect and melting of the snow glaciers more rapidly. They had to provide a place of worship in accordance with the Sikh traditions, yet make it so beautiful that it would also be in harmony with the surroundings.

The roof plays the most important part in a building, especially in the mountains. The roof should be able to bear snow load extremely well, so it was decided to make the roof consisting of aluminum sheets with astrolite backing, so that it would glow like a radiant gem and capture the different hues of the sky as it changes throughout the day, especially during the pilgrimage season. After a lot of deliberation, it was decided that it should be in the form of a pentagon. The pentagon, a five-sided form, can be associated with the number 'five' such as five piaras (five beloved), five takhts, five kakkas, etc. Our gurbani is also in favour of five's as given below.

Panch tat ko tan rachio (1427)
Panch shabad jhunkar (1040)
Panch chandal nal le aya (1348)
Panch chele wus keajey rawal(155)
Panch jana sio Sung na (641)
Panch tasker dhawat rakhe (1321)
Panch dokh aadh nagar meh(975)
Panj nawjah wakhao punch (141)
Panj wakhat niwaj gujareh (24)
Panje badhe mahabali (1193)

THE GROUND FLOOR PLAN OF THE GURUDWARA

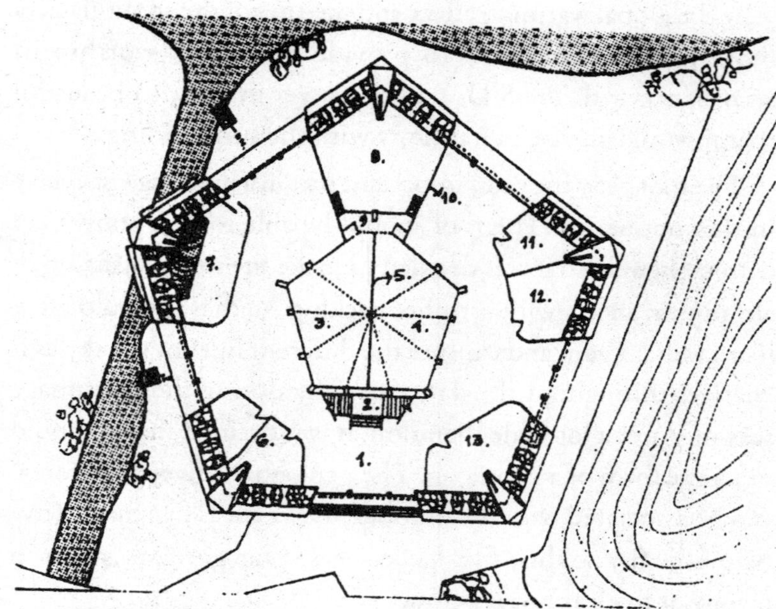

1. **Entrance Hall**
2. **Stairs leading up to the *darbar* hall**
3. **Rest Hall**
4. ***Langar* Hall**
5. **Movable partition**
6. ***Joda Ghar*** – area to keep shoes
7. **Ladies's *Paona*** – bathing area for the ladies.
8. ***Manji Sahib/Tapshila***
9. **Stairway leading down to the *Manji Sahib* from the *darbar* hall above.**
10. **Partitions blocking the *Manji Sahib* area:**

    The idea was to have the pilgrim pay obeisance here after paying their obeisance at the *darbar sahib.* Hence, the access was only from top. After completing the *parikrama* here, the pilgrim would go back upstairs from here itself.
11. **Pantry**
12. **Pressurised room** – An oxygen equipped room for the people who suffer from altitude sickness.
13. **Cloak Store**

The plan was meticulously checked out to be structurally viable after strengthening of the structural members. This was achieved by running a continuous ring that bound the structural members at various levels. This was done separately for R.C.C. and steel structures. Though there have been no earthquakes in Hemkunt itself there was a severe earthquake in Kedarnath, and the gurudwara has withstood its effect. It has further withstood weather exigencies and it has remained intact so far. At the same time it would be wise to pay special attention to its maintenance, lest the structure becomes weak from wear and tear.

As for the exact site, keeping various factors in mind, it was decided that the gurudwara should be sited near the lake and placed in a direction parallel to the nearest rising hillock. In this way the building would be shielded by the hillock in case of occurrence of avalanches. Further more, the new gurudwara should incorporate the old historical gurudwara, thus including the tapshila site of Dusht Daman. Another important factor was for the water of the lake to be diverted to the gurudwara premises for the purpose of ishnaan (sacred bath), in private for the ladies. On the right hand of the lake, a temporary structure was to be erected where men could change after ishnaan. The gurudwara consisted of two floors. The first floor consisted of the darbar hall with a corridor running all around. It had a splendid view of the surrounding snow capped mountains and it could accommodate 400-500 people sitting at one time.

The ground floor was to be used as administrative and service section containing rest hall, langar hall (community kitchen), jora ghar (place to keep shoes), ladies poana (ladies bathing place), pressurized room (room to treat patients suffering from shortage

THE FIRST FLOOR PLAN OF THE GURUDWARA

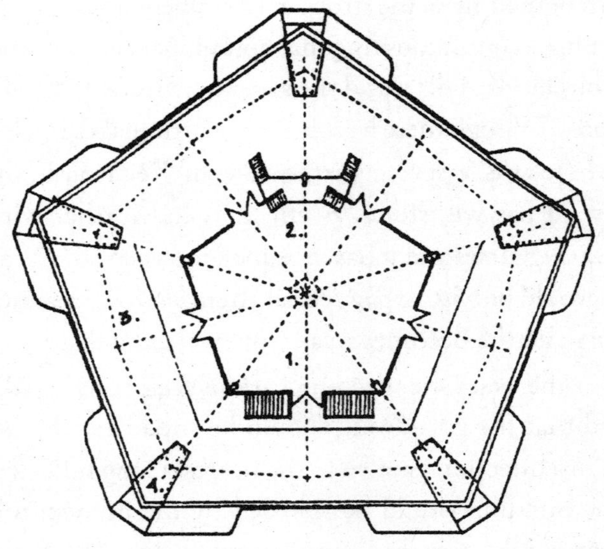

1. ***Darbar* Hall**
2. ***Darbar* Sahib**
3. Area of *parikrama.*
4. Gallery and snow chutes

of oxygen), cloakroom etc. It was decided that the old gurudwara now known as Manji Sahib, should be kept intact in such a way, that from Darbar Hall on the first floor, one steps down on the stairway to the ground floor near tapshila site, pay obeisance and after completing the parikrama come back upstairs from the opposite direction, just as it is in Sis Ganj in Delhi. No other passage has been provided to reach Manji Sahib from the ground floor.

To enhance the verticality of the elevation, roof light is provided at the top so that the incoming rays light up *Guru*

Granth Sahib from above. The chandowa (protecting shamiana) has also been suspended from the roof unlike in other gurudwaras. A Khanda (double mounted sword) is mounted at the apex. Khanda distinguishes the shrine as a gurudwara even as it forms an integral part of the gurudwara.

The building is designed in such a way that both the floors are independent. The lower floor is made of R.C.C., and the upper one is made of steel. Steel structure has to take additional pressure and impact of the snow load and the avalanches. The roof is so designed that the area of 1'x1' can bear a load of one ton of snow. The foundation and the columns were bound with R.C.C. beams all around and additional diagonal bearings were used to secure the plinth and the roof. The roof was further strengthened with the help of ties along with the pentagonal rings that bound them all in one place as one homogenous piece by welding every joint.

Mr C.P. Ghosh, an engineer from M.E.S. and Professor K.A. Patel from the School of Planning and Architecture, New Delhi were entrusted with the task of preparing the structural plan. After a number of meetings, interviews and discussions, they prepared the plan. A model of the gurudwara was prepared and displayed in New Delhi in 1967 by Brigadier Jarnail Singh Sandhu. Sangat was pleased to see this model and money started pouring in. When S. Raghbir Singh known as Kabaria saw the model, he donated Rs two lakhs on the spot for the foundation. It was estimated that the total expenses would be in the range of three to four crores and, surprisingly, the work never stopped due to the shortage of funds.

Then came the problem of transporting the building material

to the site. There is no way it can be sent on wheels all the way to Hemkunt. From Gobind Ghat to Hemkunt, the only means of transport are mules or human beings. Thus a mock up was prepared and the steel structure of the actual gurudwara to be constructed at Hemkunt was assembled at Gurudwara Rakab Ganj in New Delhi in 1967.

The yatris who have actually undertaken the journey can appreciate how difficult the terrain is. At some places the gradient is such that it is very difficult for an individual to walk. From Gobind Dham to Hemkunt the path is zigzag with hairpin bends and sometime the bend is of 180 degrees. The length of the path is sometimes not more than 4 to 5 m before it takes a U turn again. Besides, of course, all the material has to be transported up either by mules or human labour.

Considering all this, it was worked out that the length of any section should not exceed more than 2.5 m. It was further decided that since no heavy crane will be available at this height, the structural parts should be so designed that they can be hand lifted by four persons easily and then they should be bolted/ riveted/welded. This would also ensure easy negotiations around the bends. The sections were duly marked for easy identification and packed. The man who was to assemble them in Hemkunt was designated to mark them so that nothing went wrong. It was a very wise decision, because any mistake would mean so much more of hard labour of transportation besides delays. It goes without saying that at the best of times things can go wrong despite meticulous planning, and some did.

CONSTRUCTION

The construction started in July 1968. The tenders were issued all over India but due to the difficult work and terrain, no quotations were received. Ultimately the contactors S. Sahib Singh and Sant Gursharan Singh from Chandigarh turned up

Laying of roof

to take up this challenging job. The foundation stone was laid by five piaras, but on the wishes of the sangat, Nanda Singh an all time associate was also called to do the needful. A lady removed her golden ring and it was buried under the first foundation stone.

The actual problem faced for the construction of the building was the weather. The route to Hemkunt is open only from middle of June to first week of October. After October it starts snowing and all means of communication are cut off. Secondly, normally the weather is clear up to 1400 hours and then it starts raining. The high altitude effect not only reduces the working capacity of the working people but also of the machines due to lack of oxygen. The working capacity is reduced by as much as 40% as compared to the plains. There were times when the biting cold numbed the fingers of the workers. What is normally completed in one year in the plains, takes about four to five years in Hemkunt.

Quick setting cement was used, mixed in warm water. Ordinary cement would not set due to low temperatures. The phase of erection of the steel structure was the most crucial. High tensile nuts and bolts were used and the joints were welded to avoid water seepage and rusting. In spite of the fact that it was biting cold, the work was carried out to the entire satisfaction of the architect and the management.

It was indeed a Herculean task to transport the material from Gobind Ghat to Hemkunt. Because the material had to be carried by manpower or by mules, a bag of cement which normally costs about Rs 150 in the plains would cost Rs 500 or more when transported to Hemkunt. Welding machines, generators and other material had to be carried on the mules after a lot of improvisation.

M.S. Siali's book *Gurudwara in the Himalayas - Shri Hemkunt Sahib* details some of the problems encountered and the ingenuity with which they were tackled.

"The biggest challenge was the transportation of steel plates required for the foundation of the structure. Each plate, measuring 6'x 4' and about ¾ inch thick weighed 1 ton, and there were five plates. It was clear to Col M.S. Sethi, Task Force Commander of Border Roads, that the heavy load of plates had to be transported manually for a distance of nearly 15 km and from a height of 4800 ft up to a height of 15,210 ft. And that too over a narrow and difficult bridle track with steep slopes, with footprints of earlier trekkers as the only steps, hairpin bends and rickety timber bridges which were a big hindrance. Col Sethi devised L-shaped angle iron to be bolted to the plates on both the lateral sides while keeping the plates in vertical position. Two long G.I. steel pipes, one on each side of the plate, was tied to the extended portion of the 'L' of the angle irons. This arrangement provided space for 8 to 10 men on either side of the plate to put their shoulders to keep the plate about 18 inches above the ground. A reserve of 20 men followed them allowing them to change the shift after a short haulage. This enabled the carrying of five plates to the destination in about ten days."

As the work progressed, the parkash asthan of *Guru Granth Sahib* also kept changing, which was carried out as per custom and tradition of Sikhism.

The work was contracted to M/s S. Sahib Singh, Harbhajan Singh and Gursharan Singh who were experienced contractors of Chandigarh. S. Gursharan Singh was the nephew of S. Sahib Singh and an experienced civil engineer. When the construction work started S. Sahib Singh was 70 years old. But in spite of his old age he worked at that height with devotion, great zeal and enthusiasm. He was born in 1898 at Shri Nankana Sahib. Being a trustee, he had other responsibilities also such as arranging material for langar and collection of funds from Punjab. He was an experienced engineer who could correctly interpret engineering drawings and was expert in improvisation since in spite of best efforts and planning some material never reached or got misplaced. Under his able guidance, however, the work progressed according to schedule. He died a satisfied man in 1996 at the ripe age of 98.

It was decided that Deodar timber was to be used for flooring. Timber is the best material in the hills, as weather has no effect on it and it would provide insulation against outside atmosphere. This system is adopted in hill stations – to use wooden layering inside even if there are bricks or stone walls outside. Now it was a problem to get such a large quantity of seasoned timber. So they bought timber from a discarded ship which was in the process of being dismantled in Gujarat Dismantling Yard and was carried to the site. All the gurudwaras in the plains are made of marble and some people, without knowing the difference between plains and mountains, keep on giving donations for marble.

Within a space of fifty years, after the discovery of the place by Sant Sohan Singh, a pentagonal modern gurudwara, supposed to be the highest building in the world (except Tibet), has come into existence. A lot of teamwork has gone into the construction of the gurudwara and with the blessings of Wahe Guru it could be completed.

In spite of being open for four months only in a year, lakhs of people go to pay their homage.

the beauteous mountains

Though Sikhs have been making the pilgrimage to Hemkunt Sahib by the lakhs, and the numbers are still growing, these mountains have been frequented by nature-lovers down the centuries. The religious minded Hindus have their tiraths on the hills, but tourists also love to wander and admire nature's bounties. One of the places that cannot and should not be missed is the Valley of Flowers.

The Valley of Flowers is world famous and lots of tourists and admirers come here to see nature's own garden. From Gobind Dham on the way to Hemkunt, after about 800 metres, the path bifurcates. The right hand path leads to Hemkunt whereas the left one leads to the Valley of Flowers. The path is similar to that of Hemkunt but is not very steep. Before starting, observe that the weather is clear, only then take the journey. As a precaution carry some light refreshment as there are no shops on the way. The best season is mid August to mid September when the valley is in bloom. But the journey can be undertaken at any time between May to October, when there is no snow.

It is mentioned in the olden books that the valley of flowers was called Nandan Kanan and Gandh Madan. Except the locals no outsider was aware of this place. By chance in 1931, a Britisher named Frank Smythe found himself in this beautiful garden. He was returning after scaling Kamet peak, and lost his way. He reached this valley and was amazed to see the variety of scented flowers in full bloom. He stayed on for sometime at that place and collected seeds of the flowers and took them to England. In 1937, he again visited the place and after spending some time, wrote a book called *Valley of Flowers.* Because of this book, many people, nature lovers, botanists, and tourists started visiting this place and it became a highlight point on the tourist map of the world.

A glacial corridor, the valley of flowers measures eight kilometres in length and two kilometres in width and is surrounded by mountains on three sides. It stands between 3500

meters to 4000 m above sea level. Besides flowers it is a home of many wild animals, birds and butterflies of different colours. Some flowers are intoxicating and poisonous.

Probably nowhere in the world are there so many varieties of flowers in one place. It is another one of the mysteries of nature that such a beautiful valley exists right next to Hemkunt Sahib, the abode of Dusht Daman.

Life of the flowers also varies. Some bloom just for a few hours and some stay in bloom for days. A variety of ferns and wild roses can be seen on the way and in the valley. It is astonishing that the valley looks like a vast and well-tended garden, even though no one cultivates the flowers or looks after them except nature. When it snows, all the plants are buried underneath and turn into the best brand of organic manure. Once the snow melts and the sun shines the seeds or tubers sprout into plants and flowers. Probably over the years, cross breeding has taken place and new varieties of plants have come up. One can find flowers such as Himalayan blue poppy, rare varieties of primula and orchids, campanulas and many more.

In 1982, the smallest park spanning 87.5 sq km was designated as a national park. There are many streams and waterfalls adding glamour to the valley. It seems that the mountains all around are there to protect the valley and the glaciers, and the streams and waterfalls are there to beautify and irrigate it.

The only structure in the park is the grave of a British lady. Ms Jean Margert Legge, who was superintendent of a botanical garden in England. She came here with Mrs Smith, the wife of a missionary in Ranikhet, Almora (Uttaranchal) for research. She fell in love with this place and started spending one month in a year here. She compiled an Encyclopedia on flowers, illustrating it with colorful sketches. Once while collecting floral specimen from a gorge, she slipped and died on the spot. She was buried in this valley and people go and pay their homage to this great botanist.

When one visits Hemkunt, one must spare some time to visit this valley also, besides perhaps continuing to Badrinath, one of the four Dhams established by Adi Shankaracharya in India which is only 28 km ahead of Gobind Ghat. The other Dhams are Jagan Nath (Orrisa), Dwarka (Gujarat) and Rameshwaram (Tamil Naidu). It is the only Dham in Uttaranchal state.

It is situated at a height of 3110 m or 10,248 ft above sea level. It is surrounded by mountains and is situated on the right bank of river Alakhnanda. It has been said that "there are many sacred spots of pilgrimage in the heaven, earth and other parts of the world but none is equal to Badrinath nor shall there be any."

This is a sacred place and is Tap Asthan of 'Nar Narayan' who is said to be an incarnation of Vishnu. The temple, 15 m in height built in the form of a cave with a small cupola and a gilt bull and spire has been renovated several times following damages by avalanches and earthquakes.

There are 15 idols in the temple complex, finely sculpted in black stone. The Badrinath (Vishnu) image is one metre high. Other images include those of Laxmi (Vishnu's consort), Shiva, Parvati, Ganesh and Garud, (Vishnu's mount), etc.

Like other temples, this temple is very small inside and one can see hundreds of devotees standing in a long queue for darshan. By paying money (gratification), one can easily have the darshan and do puja. A common man can have darshan for a few seconds only as security people keep on pushing you out to make room for other pilgrims. Prasad normally consists of raw rice, gram dal and fresh tulsi leaves.

The doors of the temple open at six in the morning and close at one in the afternoon. It again opens at four in the evening and closes at nine at night. During winter, the idols are taken to Joshimath and the doors of the temple are closed after lighting a jyot (earthen pot full of ghee with a lighted cotton wick inside). It is said that when the doors of the temple are opened in summer then the flame of the jyot is still burning.

There are many tourist spots in and around Badrinath, to make a round of which at least two days are required. There are two natural sulphur hot springs called Tapt Kund and Narad Kund. Tapt Kund is on the bank of the river Alakhnanda, where it is customary to bathe before entering Badrinath temple. However tired one may be, while taking a bath in the kund, one feels very light and comfortable. It is said that it is good for some skin diseases and rheumatic pains.

Mana, the last Indian village, is three kilometres ahead of Badrinath. The metalled road ends in this village, though there are many army posts ahead of the village. The village is inhabited by an Indo-Mongolian tribe. Earlier this was the established route for pilgrimage to Kailash Mansrovar and rishis and munis (saints) used to trek on this route. But after China occupied Tibet, this route was closed and now one has to go via Dharchula and Lipu Lekh pass (Kumaon) and that also under government supervision. Three kilometres from Mana is the source of Sarasvati river, a glacier. The meeting of Sarasvati and Alakhnanda is called Keshav Paryag.

Vasudhara, about 8 km from Badrinath, is a magnificent waterfall of great height. It is a place worth visiting.

The pyramidal shaped snow peak (6957 m) towering above Badrinath is Neelkanth, a dramatic sight which underscores the beauty and awe of the mountains. It is best seen in the mornings as later on it could be covered with fog and clouds. Gleaming under the light of the full moon, as though shielding the temple, it is unforgettable. No wonder it is popularly known as Garhwal Queen.

Another easily accessible spot only 1.5 km away is a boulder giving an impression of the legendary snake, better known as Sheshnag, the many-headed serpent associated with Lord Vishnu. Alka Puri, 15 km from Badrinath, is the source of Alakhnanda river from the glacier snouts of Bhagirath, Khakar and Santo Path glaciers. In Hindu mythology this region is supposed to be the abode of Kuber, Yakshas and Gandharvas.

Whoever the Gods, these mountains have an aura of the divine. They have beckoned the devotee from time immemorial. And they will continue to do so for all time to come.

events – hemkunt sahib

1843	Santokh Singh	He described the events of *Bachitar Natak* in *Suraj Parkash* in Volume 14, Raas 11, Anshu 51 to 53.
1884	Bhai Tara Singh	Published *Gur Tirath Sangrah* in which Narotam gave an account of Narotam i.e. 508 Gurudwaras including details about Hemkunt along with (a sketch map showing the exact location and surruondings.
1925	Bhai Vir Singh	In his book *Kalgidhar Chamatkar* wrote an article called 'Hemkunt to Sachkhand' which became the basis of the search forHemkunt.
1932	Sant Sohan Singh	Read *Kalgidhar Chamatkar* and decided to go in search of Hemkunt Parbat.
1933	—	Read *Bachitar Natak*. Went for the search but failed in the mission.
1934	—	Located Hemkunt Parbat with the help of Rattan Singh Chuhan and Nanda Singh. Informed people in Mussoorie, Punjab but no one encouraged him. Met Bhai Vir Singh who promised to help him.
1935	—	Purchased the material. Met Havildar Modan Singh. Went to Hemkunt. Contract for the construction of the gurudwara given to Ganga Singh Bhandari of Joshimath.

Nov	—	Completed 10'x10' Gurudwara with 3' verandah 1936.
Sep	—	*Guru Granth Sahib* presented by Bhai Vir Singh was taken to Hemkunt in 1937 as per tradition assisted by Nanda Singh and installed in the Gurudwara.
1938	Havildar Modan Singh	Retired from army service and joined full time with Sohan Singh.
Feb	Sant Sohan Singh	Died in Amritsar due to tuberculosis.
1939	Havildar Modan Singh	Took over the complete work and used to spend the night at Ghagria (later named as Gobind Dham) in the hollow of a tree trunk. Bhai Vir Singh published the news about the sacred place in *Khalsa Samachar* and appealed for funds.
1942	Ghagria	Awarded the contract to Nanda Singh for Rs 400 for the construction of the Dharamshala.
1943	Gobind Ghat	Purchased 50'x50' land from Natha Singh for Rs 150.
1944-45	—	Constructed a Dharamshala consisting of two rooms.
Aug	Hemkunt	First Akhand Path by Dr. Tara Singh, Havildar Modan Singh and two other persons.
1950		Road was constructed upto Chamoli.
1951	Master Karam Singh	Went all alone for reconnaissance as instructed by Bhai Vir Singh Singh for taking jathas in future.
1952	—	Took first jatha for darshan to Hemkunt.
1953	—	Took the second jatha consisting of 30 persons.
1954	Gobind Dham	Awarded the contract to Hyat Singh for the construction of the track to Hemkunt at the rate of Rs. 200 per furlong. Total cost Rs 5000.

		Karam Singh lead the jatha consisting of 100 persons and had no problem in reaching Hemkunt.
1955	Master Karam Singh	Lead the fourth jatha.
1956		Lead the fifth jatha.
1957	Bhai Vir Singh	Died and it was a big blow to the Sikhs and especially to the Hemkunt project management.
1959	Joshimath	Purchased the land at the cost of Rs 4,200.00 for gurudwara Hemkunt.
		Approximately 1000 yatris reached to pay their homage.
1960	Mai Ram Kaur	Guru Gobind Singh came in a dream and ordered her to proceed to Hemkunt and start a gurudwara which should be the highest in the world. It was decided to construct Bhai Vir Singh Niwas Asthan.
1960	Hav Modan Singh	Formed Hemkunt Trust consisting of seven members.
1960	—— do ——	Died in Ludhiana on 25th December.
1962	Gobind Dham	Foundation stone for gurudwara laid after demolition of Dharamshala.
1962	Piplikot to Joshimath	Road constructed upto Joshimath. Joshimath Gurudwara completed under the supervision of Sant Thandi Singh and named Dusht Daman.
1964	Rishikesh	Purchased 40 bighas of land from Ram Murthy for gurudwara. Construction of road started from Joshimath to Badrinath.
1965	Gobind Dham	Completed the construction of gurudwara under the supervision of Sant Thandi Singh. First Granth Sahib Parkash.

1965	Sant Thandi Singh	Died on 1st March.
1966	Srinagar	Land purchased for gurudwara and construction work started.
1966	Hemkunt	Guru Gobind Singh's 300 birth anniversary. Programme started from Hemkunt. It was decided to construct a new and modern Gurudwara. Major General Harkirat Singh volunteered to prepare the plans taking various factors into consideration.
1967	ManMohan Singh Siali	Was appointed the chief architect. Prepared all the drawings which were approved by Hemkunt Trust.
1968	Hemkunt	Foundation stone laid by five piaras and Nanda Singh for construction of the five-faced Gurudwara.
1982	Valley of Flowers	Declared a National Park.

BIBLOGRAPHY

1. Baghel Singh, Subedar, *Shri Hemkunt Sahib.*
2. Bains, Major Umrao Singh, *Shri Hemkunt Sahib di Aloiak, Akath and Amar Katha.*
3. Bhagat Puran Singh ji Bani, *Shri Hemkunt Sahib, Ithas and Yatra Guide.* Pingalwara, Amritsar.
4. Bhangu, Bhai Rattan Singh, Shri Guru Panth Parkash.
5. Chiber, Bhai Kesar Singh, *Bansawali Nama Dasan Guran Da.*
6. *Dasam Granth, Bachittar Natak.*
7. Gurinderpal Singh, *Yatra Tap Asthan Shri Hemkunt Sahib,* Amritsar.
8. Gyani Gyan Singh, *Panth Parkash,* Bhasa Vibhag Patiala (1987).
9. Harbans Singh, *The Encyclopedia of Sikhism.* Punjabi University, Patiala, 1996.
10. Kahan Singh, Bhai, *Mahan Kosh.* Nabha National Book Shop.
11. Michaud, Heather, *Yatra Sri Hemkunt Sahib-The Sacred journey and Sacred Place.* Canada.
12. Mukhbandh (Dr Balbir Singh), *Tatkara Dasam Granth-* Bhai Bhagwant Singh Hari.
13. Nanda Singh, Bhai, *Garhwal - The Dev Bhoomi. Nest and Wings,* New Delhi.
14. Partap Singh, Master, *Merian Parbhat Pherian.* National Book Shop.

15. Sailani, Sohan Singh, *Hemkunt Guide*. Takht Shri Kesgarh Sahib.

16. Sangat Singh, J.P., *Bachittar Natak*.

17. Santokh Singh, Bhai, *Shri Gur Pratap Suraj Granth*. Amritsar, 1927-33.

18. Manmohan Siali, Singh - Architect, *Gurdwara in Himalayas-Shri Hemkunt Sahib*.

19. *Shri Hemkunt Singh Di Pawan Yatran* (*1952-1991*), Chief Khalsa Diwan Kanpur.

20. Tara Singh (Pandit Tara Har Narotam), *Gur Tirath Sangrah*.

21. Dr Tara Singh, *Shri Hemkunt Darshan*. Nahan, Himachal Pradesh.

22. Umesh Vibaghiya, *Mahabharat*. Acharya, APKS Vishvidalaya, Jaipur.

23. Uppal, Gyani Harbans Singh, *Dushat Daman Parkash*.

24. Vir Singh, Bhai, *Shri Guru Kalgidhar Chamatkar* 1.

Report from Chief Khalsa Diwan, Amritsar - "First yatra by Karam Singh."

Personal Interviews with many Gurmukhs who had undertaken this yatra.